Broken to Brave

Allowing God to Heal the Broken Places and Becoming Who He Created You to Be

Laura Horsch

Broken to Brave

www.LauraHorsch.co

For privacy reasons, some names, locations, and dates may have been changed.

Published with help from 100X Publishing, www.100xpublishing.com

ISBN Paperback: 979-8-9956258-0-3

"*Broken to Brave* by Laura Horsch is more than a story, it's a call to transformation. I've had the privilege of witnessing Laura's journey firsthand. What once marked her life no longer defines her. She has walked through deep places of brokenness, surrendered them to God, and now lives with a courage, identity, and freedom that is both authentic and powerful.

This book is a beautiful testimony of God's redeeming power. Through Laura's vulnerability and truth, she creates space for readers to encounter their own healing. It doesn't just inspire, it invites you to confront what's been hidden and step into the freedom that has always been available to you.

Laura's voice carries both compassion and conviction. If you want to stir your faith, challenge your limitations, and remind yourself that God still restores, redeems, and makes all things new, read on.

You were never meant to stay broken! This book will help you become brave."

—Cathy Greer Founder, Cathy Greer Consulting
www.cathygreer.com and Mission Support Network
www.msnministries.org

Firstly, what an honor to write an endorsement for you, beautiful Laura. I'm grateful to witness your broken to brave story so far! Everyone will identify themselves in your journey, and with Scripture alongside practical gentle questions and bringing everything back to God, it is a true blessing to read.

Most importantly, as a friend, to read YOUR story, testimony, and vulnerability fills my heart with absolute joy. With this breakthrough I can't wait to see more BOLD adventures that our Father has planned for the readers and for you, precious sister. You have a blueprint. Well done, and love always.

—Shan Ives, Christian Business Mentor,
God Morning Sisters

For everyone reading these pages,
may you feel how deeply God delights in you.

Above all, for God,
who met me in the stillness,
wrapped His arms around me,
and let me know He delights in me too.

Table of Contents

Foreword

By Melissa Hughes

I'm not sure I've ever met someone who hasn't gone through a season of brokenness in their life. In fact, I listen to people's stories for my job. It never ceases to amaze me what women walk through to get to the other side—the resilience they discover within themselves, the courage they muster when everything feels impossible, and the transformation that emerges from their most challenging moments.

When I met Laura, I knew she had a story to tell, and she came to me looking for support around her message. Whenever I sit down with someone to help them clarify the message they have inside them, I usually start with this one question, "So, what's your story?"

Whenever I ask this, the same blank stare and question comes back every time:

"Um, okay, where should I start?"

My reply is always, "Start with whatever feels like a good place to start."

I know it's a vague question. I know they're coming to me because in some ways, they are lacking clarity on what their story really is. But the reason why I lead with that is because it's always interesting to me where they begin. The starting point someone chooses reveals so much about what they consider most significant, what has shaped them most profoundly, or what they're still processing. It's like watching someone select which thread to pull first in unraveling the tapestry of their life.

Now, sometimes this single question ignites a 90-minute Zoom call of the person sharing every detail about their childhood, how they grew up, what happened in their twenties, thirties, and beyond! Or it can be more of a 15-minute life recap and I'm pulling for information. Either way, I'm always watching to see where people camp out in the details of their story. Or where they struggle to talk about certain things or what they light up talking about. These moments of hesitation or animation signal to me what's important.

For Laura, when I asked her this question, I noticed two things.

She didn't get into much of the emotional details of what she walked through, but she sure did get emotional talking about being a mom. And when I say emotional, boy, she lit up talking about her kids. I can still picture it— that genuine smile would spread across her face when she started talking about that season of her life. Suddenly, this woman who had been a bit "matter of fact" about painful situations became soft and reminiscent on those years.

I started to see that this work she was doing around her story wasn't just for herself; it was bigger than that. It was revealing her heart for moms. The feeling of, *If only I had known what I know now back then.* The desire for women to have this relationship with God sooner. As much as motherhood fills parts of who you are, I could see how what she had found in God was something she wanted for her younger self. She was standing up for her younger self—the girl who needed someone to tell her she was worthy, that she mattered, that her pain wasn't the end of her story. It's for the women who find themselves in a season of searching for love in all the wrong places, making choices out of desperation rather than wholeness. It's for the women and mothers who need a mentor they can look to, someone who has walked through the fire and emerged not unscathed, but transformed.

As we worked together, I started to realize Laura wasn't unemotional about her past; she was learning how to allow herself to feel. For so long, survival had meant keeping certain doors closed, certain memories at bay. But now, in this season of her life, she was doing the brave work of opening those doors, one by one, and letting the light in. She started calling me "Melissa the miner" whenever I would dig a little bit deeper into a memory she would share! It became our inside joke, but there was truth in it. I was mining for gold—the precious insights and lessons buried beneath layers of pain and protection.

Then, as I kept digging and pulling parts out of her story, I saw how she was allowing herself to not only see the brokenness she walked through but simultaneously step further into who God was creating her to be today. It was like watching someone shed an old skin, revealing this beautiful and authentic person underneath. She wasn't running from her past anymore; she was integrating it, learning from it, and allowing it to become part of her testimony rather than her prison.

The transformation wasn't instantaneous or easy. I'd ask her a question, and we sat in silence for a bit as she processed it. There were moments when tears flowed freely as she gave herself permission to grieve what was lost. But there were also breakthrough moments—beautiful instances when you can see someone's perspective shift, when they suddenly understand something about themselves or their journey that had been hidden before. And increasingly, there were moments when that same light I saw when she talked about her children started to come on when she talked about her own journey, her own growth, her own story.

Then, when she told me she was writing a book and asked me to read some of it, I thought, *Laura, that's brave!* Especially because she's not one to divulge information. I'll never forget reading one of the chapters and being absolutely captivated. I felt like I was right there with her as she described the scene, the emotions, the tension, and the lessons God taught her. Her writing and ability to "paint a picture" in your mind had a raw authenticity that you can't manufacture; it only comes from someone who has done the deep internal work and is willing to be vulnerable on the page.

What struck me most was how she balanced honesty about her struggles with hope about her healing. She didn't sugarcoat the difficult parts or pretend that faith made everything easy. Instead, she showed the messy, complicated reality of walking through brokenness while holding onto God. She let readers see her doubts, her failures, her moments of despair—and then she showed them how grace met her there, how redemption was possible even in the darkest valleys.

She has done the work to not just walk through brokenness and survive it. She has allowed it to be a message that brings breakthrough to others. And that's the difference between someone who has simply endured hardship and someone who has been transformed by it. Laura didn't just get to the other side; she turned around and became a guide for others still making the journey.

I've always felt that the weight behind someone's message is the experience they've walked through to get that wisdom. You can tell when someone is speaking from theory versus lived experience. There's a depth and an authenticity that can't be replicated. Laura carries a weighty message around helping women go from broken to brave. Not because of how articulate she is, though she certainly has a gift with words. Not because she has all the answers, because she would be the first to tell you she doesn't. But because she has walked the walk. She has been in the pit, felt the despair, made the mistakes, and found her way to healing and wholeness.

Her message resonates because it's earned. Every word comes from a place of hard-won wisdom. Every encouragement is backed by personal experience. Every promise of hope is rooted in her own journey from darkness to light. When Laura tells you that healing is possible, that you can move from broken to brave, that your past doesn't have to define your future, believe her, because she's living proof.

I know this book will encourage you. I know this was written from her heart. I know this book carries stories, lessons, and vulnerability that will help you see God in whatever broken place you might find yourself today. Whether you're struggling with past trauma, current challenges, or fears about the future, Laura's story will meet you where you are. Her honesty will give you permission to be honest with yourself. Her courage will inspire your own. Her faith will strengthen yours.

I know this book will help you to not feel so alone and see that someone is cheering you on from the other side. Because that's what Laura does best: she shows up for women who are still in the midst of their struggle and says, "I see you. I've been there. And I'm here to tell you that there is hope, there is healing, and there is a beautiful life waiting for you on the other side of this brokenness."

So, as you turn these pages, know that you're not just reading a book; you're receiving an invitation. An invitation to be honest about your own brokenness, to believe that transformation is possible, and to take the brave steps toward the life God has for you. Laura has walked this path, and now she's extending her hand to walk alongside you.

—Melissa Hughes, Founder & CEO Rise Agency
www.melissaleahughes.com

A Letter to the Reader

Writing a book was never part of my plan. It stemmed from a newfound desire to be radically obedient to God's voice. Once I made the decision to obey Him, there was no turning back—not even when He told me to write a book.

I believe this book found its way into your hands as part of God's plan as well. Healing and a deeper intimacy with my Heavenly Father came through writing these pages. And I believe there are others God wants to draw nearer to Him through the words that follow.

Like everyone, I have had painful experiences in my life. I learned early on that it was best to tuck my feelings and circumstances into the corners of my heart, where I didn't have to deal with them and could pretend they didn't exist. What I didn't realize at the time was that instead of brushing things off, I was building walls around my heart—walls designed to protect me from getting hurt. Unfortunately, those same walls meant to keep the pain out also kept the love out.

I didn't give it much thought then. It was as though I had programmed myself to be strong. "Suck it up, buttercup" could have been my motto because that's what I learned to do. *Suck it up. Keep going. Strive and push through.* This mindset brought me a lot of success, but it never got me peace.

Then one day, God placed a beautiful soul in my life who guided me on a journey of healing. I'll never forget the day Cathy described it as God holding one of my hands while she held the other, walking me through the process. If I'm being honest, there were times they didn't just walk me through it, they *dragged* me through it. And there were moments when they carried me.

That journey didn't just bring healing; it gave my pain purpose. I could finally recognize some of the places where God had been with me, even when I didn't see Him at the time. It was a beautiful adventure—one I wouldn't trade for anything. There are days I wish I had taken the journey 30 years earlier, knowing the impact it would have on the rest of my life. But that wasn't the story God wrote for me, so I trust that He has a plan in all of it, even when I can't see the whole picture this side of heaven. He is faithful and just, and I am filled with anticipation for where He will lead me next. Because now I can see that He has been with me all along.

Today, I find myself in a place of peace instead of chaos, of surrender instead of striving, and it feels so good. As I learned how to be still in His presence, God met me right there in my living room chair and held me tight. Although I had always known God loved me—maybe because He *had to*—for the first time in my life, I knew that God delighted in me. Not because of anything I had done or failed to do, but because of who He is.

My prayer for you is that somewhere within these pages, God will meet you in the stillness of His presence. In those moments, healing begins and identity and purpose are revealed. When you finally realize that God loves you not because of what you have done but despite it, you can begin to walk in boldness and faith. And when we surrender our will for His, we begin to operate in His power.

Always remember this: you are a daughter of the King and Creator of all things, and that makes you royalty. So, pick up your crown, dust it off, and learn to walk with the authority you have as a daughter of God. Be still and listen. Allow Him to direct your path. And when He speaks, respond with radical obedience.

Love ya!

Laura

ONE

Created on Purpose

When you've been close to death as many times as I have and you're still alive, there's something bigger at work.

My parents were 21, and my brother Jason had just turned four when I was born. The first six months of my life had to have left my parents wondering what they were thinking when they decided to have another baby. If you are a parent, you know what I am talking about.

Rachael, my first child, was a very content baby. I'm sure part of what helped shape those memories is that it's easier to be well-rested when you have an infant, especially if you are blessed to take maternity leave and family medical leave. Getting up in the middle of the night for feedings and diaper changes doesn't have the same effect on a person when you don't have to rush out of the house right away in the morning.

Do you remember what it's like getting up with your toddler the morning after a sleepless night with an infant? It's something hard to forget. Now picture that for several consecutive months!

With that in mind, the first six months of my life were quite the interruption to the life my parents had previously known. What my mom initially presumed was a little stomach bug turned into several months of doctor's appointments. I couldn't keep anything down. The small-town doctors didn't know why I kept throwing up, but they assumed it had something to do with a milk allergy or intolerance of some sort. They kept sending my mom home to try different formulas, including soy milk and even Jell-O water, but nothing worked.

How scary it must be to watch your infant constantly sick and continuing to lose weight, not getting any answers, not being able to do anything about it, all while at the brink of exhaustion. Finally, someone told my mom she should try this doctor in a larger nearby city. Thankfully, within what seemed like five minutes with the new doctor, he diagnosed me with a yeast infection that had spread through my entire body, including my stomach and intestines. If she had brought me in another day or two later, I probably wouldn't have survived.

God answered my family's prayers, and my life was spared. I wish it were my only close call with death, but it was only one of many.

As a child, I loved the outdoors. My sister Christy was born when I was three and Jason was seven. Remembering how stressful being a mom can be, and because my brother was four years older than I, I can imagine my mom telling him to *go play outside...and take Laura with you* more often than not. We were always outside. Many of my childhood memories included Jason and me finding ways to entertain ourselves in the yard. I'm assuming partly because he had to and partly because he could choose to play with me or by himself.

I remember winter memories of digging in the snow and creating forts with tunnels we could climb in and out of. Another one of our favorite winter activities was sledding down the big hill behind our house. Usually, our parents would bring us there because the river separated our home from the sledding hill. When you live next to a river, and you are eight years old, you have it cemented into your head that the river isn't safe.

I recall bits and pieces of a particular winter day when I was four. My brother, the great trouble-shooter that he was, was determined to find a safe (in his eight-year-old mind) way to get across the river that kept us from the thrill of sledding on an otherwise typical winter day. Then, it came to him! He just needed to throw rocks on the ice to see if it was safe enough to walk across. SUCCESS! It was solid enough to hold the stones, so it must be thick enough to cross. But just to be extra safe, one should cross the river lightest to the heaviest, because if the ice cracks at all when the lighter person is on the ice, it wouldn't be safe for the heavier one.

Fortunately, I was light enough to keep the ice from breaking underneath me. However, I managed to step onto a piece of ice that was too small to stay in place. I clearly remember the sheet of ice acting like a teeter-totter when the person on the bottom jumped off abruptly. Instead of banging my bottom on the ground, I slid down the ice and right into the river, feeling the current pulling at my feet. I'm not sure how, but my brother pulled me out of the water before I went over my waist and helped me up to the house.

Another near-death experience. God was definitely watching over me, which I can clearly see now, but at four years old, it was just something that kept us from reaching our mission of getting to the sledding hill. Looking back, I can see how even those early moments instilled in me a sensitivity to life that carried over into the years ahead.

As a child, I often found myself feeling deeply, as if others never did. Some may have concluded it was trauma from the past, but I realize now I have always been empathetic. At 14, my best friend told me she wanted to die and had taken a lot of Tylenol the previous night because she hated her life. She told me several times how she had attempted to take her life. That news left me hurting—not only for her, but also for myself, knowing our friendship wasn't enough of a desire for her to live. *Our friendship doesn't bring her any joy* was my interpretation at the time, which was actually a spirit of rejection.

For some reason, at 14, these words deeply affected me and motivated me to take action—an action which I would later regret. My action? I decided to do to her what she had done to me, so I took a bunch of Tylenol that night. Why? *Then she will know exactly how I felt.* She would be in my shoes. However, after taking all the Tylenol, I didn't have the same reaction that she did. I couldn't go to school the next morning because I couldn't stop throwing up. I suddenly realized what I had done. Fearful of telling my parents, I confided in my brother who happened to be visiting, and he brought me to the hospital.

At the hospital, I still couldn't stop throwing up. Nurses inserted a tube through my nose and down into my stomach. I vividly remember gagging and trying to pull the tube back out as that reflex started. After a couple of attempts, it was in place. I guess I told them about my friend's attempt and mine, because before I knew it, she was in my room being treated for the same thing. She was fine and released; however, I spent a couple of days in the local hospital before the doctor told my parents there was nothing more they could do. I was not doing well. A spirit death was after me again.

Believing they might lose me, my parents asked the priest to come and give me the last rites. An ambulance transported me to the children's hospital, where the doctors worked quickly, and I made an unexpected recovery. Walking back into school not long after, I carried with me the sobering truth that God had intervened in my life once again.

These experiences made me realize a spirit of death was trying to take me out, but God wouldn't allow it. He had a plan for my life, as He does for us all. We are all given a unique purpose. And as I look back, I can see how those early brushes with death shaped the way I would come to view life, faith, and purpose.

For me, discovering my God-given purpose has been the key to confidence—not in myself, but in Him. This kind of confidence is something you can carry with you into every circumstance life brings. There's a steady strength in knowing He made you, He goes before you, He is with you, and He provides what you need. The Cambridge Dictionary defines purpose as "why you do something or why it exists," and it adds that doing something on purpose means doing it intentionally, not by accident. That makes my favorite reminder even more powerful:

You were created on purpose (not by accident), for a purpose (you exist to do something), for such a time as this (right now).

Discovering Purpose

Here are a few steps to help you discover your purpose.

1. Start with God.

It's essential to start with the One who created you. Spend time in prayer, asking God to show you how He uniquely designed you. Just remember that after we ask God something, we need to BE STILL and listen. God speaks to us in different ways. Be open to different ways

He may speak, and see how you hear Him best! For me, it's while journaling.

2. Make a list.

Make a list of the things that bring you joy and sadness. Part of the uniqueness God created you with are your feelings, emotions, likes, and dislikes. Things that move us deeply are connected to the assignments God has planned for you. Write down the things you are passionate about because it's not by accident that they move you.

3. Write down your strengths.

Along with our emotions, we have all been given gifts (both physical strengths and spiritual gifts) that God has given us to prepare us for our calling and to serve others. The Bible says, "God has given each of you a gift from his great variety of spiritual gifts. Use them well to serve one another" (1 Peter 4:10 NLT). It can be helpful to ask for input from those closest to you.

4. Reflect on your journey.

One of the most powerful ways I've heard this put is: *"God does to you what He wants to do through you."*

I was reminded of this today while talking with a friend about how she uniquely serves others. Her husband passed away a couple of years ago, and she shared how, when another friend lost her husband, she sent her a message every morning for a month, walking with her through the ache of grief.

Doing this would never have crossed my mind because I haven't walked in those same shoes. But for her, it flowed naturally out of her own journey. Our own unique experiences help shape us and prepare us for our calling.

Verses

Ephesians 2:10 (ESV)
"For we are his workmanship, created in Christ Jesus for good works, which God prepared beforehand, that we should walk in them."

Jeremiah 1:5 (AMP)
"Before I formed you in the womb I knew [and] approved of you [as My chosen instrument], and before you were born I separated [and] set you apart, consecrating you; [and] I appointed you as a prophet to the nations."

Being spared for a reason doesn't mean we automatically know how to honor that reason. As my family worked hard to build a life, I began to learn an unexpected lesson—one about time, attention, and the quiet cost of always doing *more*.

TWO

The Cost of Busyness

We're all busy. But if we're not careful, busyness becomes the enemy of *presence*.

We say we're doing it for our families—working harder, taking on more, building a future. But sometimes the cost of busyness is the very people we love most.

My parents were high school sweethearts and married when they found out my brother was on the way. My mom had just turned 17, and my dad wasn't far behind. One unique thing about my parents is that they have two anniversaries just a few days apart. Because my dad was only 16, he wasn't old enough to marry in Minnesota. Their first anniversary marks the day they drove to South Dakota to get married legally. Three days later, they were married in a Catholic church in Minnesota.

I don't know about you, but I can *feel* the tension that must have filled the car as my mom, her parents, my dad, and his parents made the eight-hour round trip to South Dakota. I imagine the air was so thick it was hard to breathe.

Teen pregnancy is a lot more common—and accepted—now than it was then. I can only imagine the thoughts racing through my grandparents' minds. As a parent myself, I know the kind of second-guessing that comes in those moments: *What could I have done differently? What will others think?*

And while my grandparents wrestled with shame and second-guessing, my parents didn't get the luxury of wondering what might have been. They were shoved headfirst into adulthood before they were ready. My dad was still a kid in high school, and my mom had to drop out of school to raise hers. Their world was built on survival, not dreams. Starting their marriage that way gives you a sense of the financial background of my upbringing. My parents had to work hard to make ends meet. Very hard...

When I was five, my dad nearly died in a car accident. I remember bits and pieces of those days while he was home recovering. One memory is still vivid. It was a cold winter day, and my hands were frozen from playing outside. I headed straight for my parents' bedroom, knowing I'd find Dad there. He lay on the far side of the waterbed, scruffy-bearded in his white V-neck undershirt. Giggling, I tucked my little hands under his arms, letting his body heat thaw them out. The warmth flowed from my fingertips straight to my heart. Even now, this memory stirs deep emotions in me.

After months of recovery and mounting bills, Dad went back to work. To earn more, he became an over-the-road truck driver. That meant weeks away from home. With Dad gone, the weight of daily life landed on Mom's shoulders. She worked at the local Red Owl grocery store and managed the household, all while caring for three children. Additionally, my parents tilled the ground where an old barn had stood and planted a large garden. The vegetables helped feed us, but most of all, the extras could be sold for income.

She sounds busy, doesn't she? Now add a nine-year-old son and my sister and me (ages two and five) into the mix. I get tired just thinking about the cooking, cleaning, laundry, and baths, let alone finding time to play with us. My mom was burning her candle at both ends until she realized her wick was almost gone.

Something had to change. When I was ten, that change came in the form of packed boxes and a four-hour drive north to live near my grandparents. What a blessing to have my dad around again! No more being gone for weeks at a time, driving over the road to make ends meet. Things are different when dads are present; for me, that felt especially true.

I remember little things—my dad digging a pond in the sandy yard, lining it with heavy black plastic, and filling it with ducks and geese. I remember how often they "fertilized" the lawn. He also taught me to drive the Case tractor with a six-foot mower deck, and even though it took me three days to mow the grass, I felt proud to help. My dad worked alongside my grandpa, making gas deliveries and repairing small engines when he had time.

Looking back, I realize it wasn't the ducks, the tractor, or even the new business that mattered most; it was the time. Kids don't measure love in toys or money; they measure it in moments. And those moments with him were worth more than anything money could buy.

But seasons of presence don't always last. Four years later, everything changed again. My parents bought the shell of a building and started a small-engine business. With that, a new kind of business (and busyness) began.

And they thought they were busy before!

I'm sure you've been there too. For me, it was when all three of our kids were toddlers. I remember telling Nathan, "When things slow down a little bit, then we can _____." But if you've lived it, you know the truth: things don't just slow down.

The time, energy, and money that go into starting a business from scratch—especially one with overhead—is challenging enough. Add raising kids into the mix, and you can see the strain. My parents even lived in the back of the store to make it all work. But for my sister and me, it meant our parents' thoughts and attention were rarely far from business.

The business was a constant mix of blessings and heartache. I saw my parents every day, yet I still missed them. Maybe you've been there too—being with someone but still feeling alone.

Looking back, I realize my parents weren't the only ones. We all do this. We fill our lives so full that we avoid facing what matters most. For many of us, busyness becomes a distraction—even a form of escape.

What good came from their hard work? A strong work ethic was planted in me. The bad? I often felt like I wasn't as important as the business. As a teenager, how things *felt* mattered more than what I knew. And what I felt were empty bleachers and missed moments.

What I have learned is that life doesn't slow down on its own. We need to be protective of our schedules and intentional about what we put on them. Busyness is often celebrated as if it's a badge of honor. But what it can really do is rob us of the moments that matter most. Love is measured in presence, not productivity. Our families won't remember how many hours we worked or what we accomplished.

They'll remember the times we were there, *really* there, fully present. God calls us to work hard, yes, but He also tells us to be still.

Making Time Count

1. Reflect

Look at your calendar/schedule. Where are the places where busyness comes at the cost of presence? John Maxwell has an excellent resource for prioritizing tasks: Time Quadrants. This tool helped me discover where I was "wasting" time that I could reclaim and tasks I could delegate to someone else.

2. Think long term.

When weighing the importance of things on your calendar, remember to consider years and sometimes even decades down the road. A good question to ask yourself is what will matter more in ten days/ten years, this task or this person? Always prioritize people!

3. Set boundaries with busyness.

Healthy boundaries are just that...healthy! It's better to say no to something (especially after it falls short in the prioritizing process) than to overcommit and create unnecessary stress. A book that really helped me with this was *Boundaries* by Dr. Henry Cloud and Dr. John Townsend.

4. Be fully present.

Being present is definitely one area where we need to be intentional. Sometimes it means putting the phone away for a while. Don't worry about your to-do list, get rid of other distractions, and give valuable relationships your undivided attention. This is especially important when it comes to our spouses and children.

Verses

Psalm 90:12 (NIV)
"Teach us to number our days, that we may gain a heart of wisdom."

Ecclesiastes 4:6 (NLT)
"Better to have little, with quietness, than to have much with toil and chasing the wind."

Presence made me feel chosen. Absence made me feel lonely.

I didn't know it then, but I was already learning how to build small walls around my heart in order to protect myself. To swallow disappointment. To blink back tears. To make sure I never became "too much."

There was one moment—small, almost forgettable—that cemented this belief in me. One that would follow me for decades.

THREE

When Strength Meant Silence

Some of my earliest memories of my dad are a mix of diesel fumes, long roads, and longing. He was both my hero and my heartbreak.

If you ask me what one thing, if taken away, impacts a little girl the most—even a big girl—it's her daddy. That must be the reason for the saying we know so well: *Daddy's little girl.* There's a special bond between a father and daughter, one that leaves a terrible hole when love or presence is absent.

As I mentioned, I remember my dad being away for work most of the time during one season of my childhood. And I remember how happy I was when he was home. I would've done almost anything he asked to spend extra time with him. When he was away, Jason, Christy, and I found little ways to think about him—to help us forget how much we missed him.

During that season, we had what I like to call the "rat rods" of bicycles—each one a patchwork of parts from several others. It didn't matter what they looked like; we convinced ourselves they were cool. The parts we saw as less than cool, like the banana seat with the tall sissy bar (which, of course, were for sissies), were overshadowed by the playing cards clipped to the spokes with clothespins, creating the best clickety-clack soundtrack you've ever heard. When we had spare time, we'd hop on those motorless rat rods and cruise the short stretch from the end of our driveway to the interstate overpass, patiently waiting for the next semi to pass beneath us.

I could feel excitement stirring inside as a semi came into view in the distance. By the time it neared, while my brother was pumping his arm to get the driver to honk, I couldn't contain my excitement. My whole body joined in, jumping up and down with my arm. The feeling of victory would overtake us when the driver reached up to pull the cord, sounding the horn. The elation would linger as the horn's thunderous sound echoed while the tractor-trailer passed beneath the bridge we were on. The thrill would fade—until the next truck appeared on the horizon.

Another thing that helped ease the burden of missing Dad came with Alabama's new song release, "18-Wheeler." Whenever it played on the radio, the bellering began. (I say bellering because there's no way you could call what we did "singing.") My sister and I belted out every word at the top of our lungs, somehow feeling like it brought our dad closer while he was driving somewhere down the road in his own 18-wheeler. Hearing that song, to this day, puts a smile on my face.

Singing about 18-wheelers was one thing, but living the life of one, even for a few days, was another story.

When I was about seven, I finally got my chance to be with Dad out on the road—a real trucking trip—to Wisconsin, then to Michigan, or maybe the other way around. I never could keep it straight. A sense of pride welled up as I climbed into the big green cab-over tractor, its long flatbed trailer hitched. I was trucking with my dad.

Everything was perfect—except for bathroom breaks. I wasn't nearly as good at "holding it" as my dad, who I swear must have been part camel. The first time I had to climb down from the semi to go into the ditch, the tall grasses waved around me like a curtain, helping me hide my embarrassment. Thankfully, I survived that roadside potty break—the only one I remember. Either I was so horrified the first time that I learned to hold it better, or perhaps I just decided it wasn't so bad. Whatever the case, I outgrew that fear.

There was another memorable stop on our trip. This one was at a large truck stop. I strutted in beside my dad, proud to be his little trucker girl. With my short pixie cut—thanks to a do-it-yourself haircut gone wrong—and my brother's hand-me-down striped tank top, I was sure I looked the part.

As we walked in and neared the counter, I was doing the "potty dance." My dad asked the cashier where the restroom was, and as she pointed, I took off running. Moments later, I realized something was strange. *Trucker bathrooms don't look like any restroom I've seen before.* Then, I heard my dad calling my name from *inside* the bathroom. *Dad? Why are you in here?* I may have been young, but I was old enough to go trucking with my dad and to know boys don't belong in girls' bathrooms. It turns out I was in the boys' room. The first clue? Although I didn't know what they were at the time, it was the urinals on the wall. Thankfully, sometimes boys need stalls too. When I came out, the cashier sent me an apologetic look, but with my haircut and outfit, I probably would've made the same mistake.

The rest of the trip was hot and sticky, but I didn't care. With windows down and hair whipping, I was on top of the world. I loved looking out my window and seeing how much bigger we were than everyone else on the road. I'm sure we saw a couple of kids during the trip, pumping their arms with the trucker salute, trying to get us to honk our loud horn—you know, the ones who weren't big enough actually to ride in the semi with their dads!

There was something about riding in that semi with my dad that made me feel extra special—just me and my daddy cruising down the open road.

But sometimes, even the sweetest memories have a sting.

Then, it happened. One hot summer day, somewhere along a Midwestern highway, I was perched forward in my seat, looking through the windshield, taking in all of the scenery. When I slid back to switch views and look out my side window, I unknowingly sat on a bee that had flown in through the open window. *Ouch.*

I couldn't keep the tears from streaming down my face, no matter how hard I tried. As quietly as I could, I brushed away the smashed bee. My little seven-year-old mind knew one thing for sure: I couldn't let my dad see me cry. If he did, he might think I wasn't big enough to be his little trucker girl, after all. So I faced out my window, blinked away the tears, and let the wind finish drying them for me—thankful for the lull in conversation at the time.

I didn't know it then, but that small moment planted a seed: the belief that strength meant silence. The wind may have dried my tears that day, but it also carried a whisper I couldn't hear yet—a whisper that one day, strength and softness could coexist. It would take decades—and God's gentle love—to unlearn that silence.

I have often wondered why I remember the bee sting so vividly all these years. It wasn't until God revealed to me that it was foundational in the lie I believed for many decades: *to be strong means I need to be silent.* I learned not to talk about what hurt me or how I felt. The enemy would remind me that others had it worse and I should just keep quiet and be grateful for all of my blessings.

But God is showing me how He defines strength differently. Kingdom strength comes through surrender, dependence, and love. Maybe you have found yourself believing the same lie. God wants you to recognize the difference between how the world defines strength and how He does. He is calling you to find your strength in Him. Come to Him with all of your "stings" in life, and let your wounds be fully healed—as only He can do. Only then will you experience what real strength is.

Finding What You've Silenced

1. Ask God to reveal your silence.

Spend some time with God. Ask Him to reveal areas in your life where you are keeping quiet when you should be speaking up. Be still and listen for the moments He brings to mind. When were the times that you held back your words or hid your feelings when He wanted you to speak up?

2. Name what you've been holding in.

Write down the memories that come to mind—the times when you felt like you couldn't speak up or show pain. Sometimes just acknowledging the moments is the first step toward healing.

3. Notice the lies behind the silence.

For each of the above memories, ask God, "What did I believe about myself, or You, that made me stay silent?" Learning what lies you are believing will help you recognize patterns in your silence.

4. Invite God to replace the lies with truth.

Bring each of the lies you have been believing to God in prayer. Picture yourself laying each one at the foot of the cross. Replace each lie with a truth of who God says you are.

5. Practice using your voice.

Start with small steps. Spend time talking with God about how you are feeling. He knows, but there is intimacy and healing in saying it. Ask Him to give you wisdom and be your strength as you begin choosing bravery over silence.

Verses

Isaiah 40:29–31 (NLT)
"He gives power to the weak and strength to the powerless. Even youths will become weak and tired, and young men will fall in exhaustion. But those who trust in the Lord will find new strength. They will soar high on wings like eagles. They will run and not grow weary. They will walk and not faint."

Jeremiah 1:9 (NLT)
"Then the Lord reached out and touched my mouth and said, 'Look, I have put my words in your mouth!'"

When strength is defined as silence, pain doesn't disappear, it just goes underground. What followed were years of hidden fractures masked by smiles and achievements.

FOUR

The Things No One Saw

Like cracks hidden beneath ice, the fractures in my life weren't visible to anyone else. I hid behind achievements and smiles, but numbness ran deep below the surface.

If you have never experienced a Minnesota winter, the land of 10,000 frozen lakes, it's something to see, especially on some of the larger fishing lakes, like Mille Lacs Lake. Open-water fishing turns into ice-house fishing in the heart of winter. Together, many of the resorts around the lake plow hundreds of miles of roads on the ice so that people can drive to their favorite fishing spots. The lake turns into little "towns" of tiny houses scattered across the tundra that was once a lake.

It reminds me of farming communities, where fields span for miles. You can tell where the houses and un-plowable land are because that's the only place you will see trees. The only difference with the frozen lakes is that you aren't locating homesteads with trees; you can spot the fishing holes by the cluster of icehouses.

For us kids, though, the frozen roads weren't about fishing. They were an open playground and, for my brother, a tempting test track. Although my uncle and brother weren't into fishing, the frozen lake roads held a different fascination for them. Wide roads made of ice plus rear-wheel drive cars equaled the thrill of drifting and spinouts. The problem? The car Jason longed to drive on the ice was my parents' mid-1970s Oldsmobile Cutlass Supreme. He loved that car and probably imagined himself drifting through the corners on the ice, honing his driving skills.

The opportunity presented itself in the winter of 1986. My parents had an overnight commitment, and my brother was in charge of my sister and me. Stay home, take care of the girls, do your chores, don't have friends over, and stay out of trouble were the instructions he was probably given. However, the keys were in the car, and our parents were gone. Jason, in his 15-year-old mind, devised a plan; somehow, our 16-year-old uncle was included in the process. The following events are to the best of my recollection, with some assumptions on the thoughts of others involved.

Uncle Kurt came over with his sister, Karla, who was nine. I don't recall if they came over after Christy was in bed. The plan unfolded as follows: my little sister went to bed, and Aunt Karla and I could hang out, which would keep me quiet, while Uncle Kurt and Jason took the car out on the ice. I'm sure it sounded like more fun for us to go with them on a car ride, but not for the boys; instead, they had to come up with plan B to keep us busy.

Right next to our house was the shared shop my dad and grandpa ran. A portion of it was set aside for my grandpa's entertainment area. The locked room housed a couple of blackjack tables and a few slot machines. The next thing I remember is being in that room, Karla and I both sitting in front of a slot machine, being handed a pile of quarters, a couple of glasses, and a bottle of something we were far too young to be drinking. We were told to stay busy, and they would be back in a little while.

At the time, it all felt like an adventure, not a setup. But looking back as an adult, I can see Jason's pattern. It's unbelievable how we spend time looking back on events of the past and thinking, "Why couldn't I see it then?" Of course, there are many reasons, most of which can be distilled from life experience. My brother was strategic in the things he wanted to do, even when he knew he shouldn't. One of his tactics was having a cohort to share blame with. Another was making sure those left behind felt too guilty to tell. That night, his plan was simple: if Karla and I were doing something we shouldn't, we'd be less likely to rat him out.

As far as I remember, Aunt Karla and I enjoyed our evening together, but we would have enjoyed it just as much with Kool-Aid, popcorn, and a movie. It's frightening when you recognize that the enemy is lurking everywhere, just like he's portrayed in various films. I can't believe there is any other explanation for the events of that evening. However, I also know God was watching over us and protecting us through it all.

That night was my first taste of how alcohol and secrecy could mix. Unfortunately, it wouldn't be the last. Within a few years, that pattern would lead me into situations I never imagined.

My next memory with alcohol is skipping the last day of school in the 7th grade. My friend, her boyfriend, his cousin, and I went somewhere other than school and drank and hung out. They were old enough to drive and had a way of getting alcohol for us. It didn't take many more times of hanging out before I found myself in the middle of a nightmare.

One of the boys had been pressuring me to do things I clearly didn't want. I said no, but one night my resistance didn't matter. We ended up in a trailer house out in the country. My friend and her boyfriend left for another room, and I was left alone, under the influence and scared. That was the night a line was crossed. As a 14-year-old girl, something was taken from me that I could never get back.

Fifteen or so years later, that boy's name came up in conversation between my mom and me. She told me she had suspected something back then. Instead of protecting me, she had set it aside, and I carried the weight alone. Another victory for the enemy—another reason for me to believe I wasn't worth loving.

After that night, something in me shifted. I wanted to escape that boy and start fresh, but instead I stumbled into a different kind of danger. I found myself spending time with another friend who had an even older boyfriend. This led me into connections with people much older than me long before I had the maturity to handle it. My parents eventually allowed me to start dating at 14 because the boy seemed like a "nice kid."

My new freedom quickly led to more parties and "good times," until I realized I was heading down a destructive path. Unfortunately, I was too young to truly process what was happening. The next several years left me in and out of drinking, putting myself in risky and sometimes frightening situations, and locked in a cycle of using alcohol first to have fun, then to cope, and eventually to numb.

As I soon learned, moving out on my own didn't break the cycle. A few months after I turned 17, as most teenagers do, I thought I knew a lot more than my parents did. I decided (for the third time) that I was moving out. It didn't take me long to discover what my parents already knew at that age: living on your own was expensive.

Thankfully, they had instilled a strong work ethic in me, because I was going to need it.

Even with a new apartment and new independence, alcohol still had its grip on me. It was a mix of work and school during the week and parties on the weekends. By this time, I had met Nathan, so putting myself in dangerous situations was no longer an issue. But even with him, I carried more emotions than anyone my age should have to process. Alcohol had become a method to dull the feelings I wasn't prepared to deal with.

On the outside, though, no one would have guessed. By the time I graduated from high school with honors, I had a full-time job in the purchasing department of a local crating company, my own apartment, and was 12 credits away from earning an Associate's in Arts degree.

I learned from a young age that I could hide behind achievements and no one would know just how broken I was. NO ONE. No one, that is, but me.

I was once told I wasn't anyone's favorite because people knew I would always be fine. Maybe I believed that too. I let others see the best parts of my life and hid the rest behind accomplishments. But brokenness doesn't heal just because you cover it up. It lingers until you invite God in to restore what's been hidden. Our calling can't flow out of brokenness. And the truth is, someone is waiting for you to step boldly into your calling as a healed child of God so they can be blessed through you.

Giving God the Broken Pieces

1. Be honest with yourself.

Dig deep! Search for places in your life where you are performing to hide the broken places instead of allowing them to heal.

2. Face the brokenness.

Instead of avoiding pain, learn to recognize it. Healing begins with dealing with the things that cause us pain. Avoiding dealing with the pain only delays our healing.

3. Exchange with God.

Spend some time with God. Hand your broken pieces to Him. Ask Him for help in identifying any unhealed hurts from long ago that may be triggering the pain. Interestingly, many of the things that caused me pain were from triggers of unhealed pain from decades ago!

4. Identify the Lie.

Recognize how the enemy fills our minds with lies that we hold on to (and start to believe) that keep us in a place of brokenness, and replace them with God's truth. Some of the lies I had to recognize were *I'm fine*, and *I'm not worthy*.

5. Step into authenticity.

Put down the mask, and let others see the real you. The beautiful person God created, in His image, for a special calling just for you!

Verses

Psalm 147:3 (ESV)
"He heals the brokenhearted and binds up their wounds."

Psalm 34:18 (NLT)
"The Lord is close to the brokenhearted; he rescues those whose spirits are crushed."

When pain stays hidden long enough, it starts to feel ordinary. I didn't yet realize how much of my childhood I had labeled as "normal" without ever stopping to question it.

FIVE

The Becoming

Have you ever looked back at your childhood and thought, "Maybe that wasn't quite as normal as I believed it was"?

My childhood was filled with scattered memories, most of which include Jason. He was my big brother, and, being much older, he was often my built-in babysitter when we played outside. My mom had a lot on her plate and needed the help he could provide.

Looking back, I can see how these early experiences helped shape my definition of "normal." They shaped how I learned to handle fear, risk, and even belonging.

However, the quality of care from a boy that age doesn't compare to that of a teenager, for example. Let's be honest, nine-year-old Jason had some advantages and disadvantages. I recall playing in the small woods in our backyard, building forts and trails by clearing away leaves and other debris. The cleared area would be our trails and houses. The creative ways we came up with for playtime that didn't include any toys still amazes me.

The downside of nine-year-old Jason was that his logic hadn't caught up with his adventurous ways, as I mentioned when we tried to cross the river that cold winter day.

Then came the more "experienced" Jason. One might think an older brother would make wiser decisions as he grew, but let's say his creativity only expanded. There were the less-than-ideal shenanigans he conjured up with his older brain. Things like putting an aerosol can in with the papers we were burning and encouraging me to wait and watch...until he suddenly said, "Run!" At that moment, running away as fast as my preschool legs could carry me, the aerosol can shot through the air and hit my leg, as if I were the target it was aiming for.

It must have been my magnetic personality, because there was also the time he was shooting a BB gun at a big rock. I know his math wasn't so good that he could figure out the exact angle for the BB to ricochet off the rock and hit me...but it did.

Sometimes the things he came up with were just bad ideas that sounded good at the time. Like the time he coaxed me into taking an extra sissy bar from one of our "rat rods" and touching a metal grate that was leaning against an electric fence. I'll never forget how quickly the coaxing turned to "Stop crying, it didn't hurt that bad," as our parents pulled in the driveway.

It's funny now, but back then, those moments did more than leave scars and stories. They also quietly shaped my understanding of safety...and of myself.

There were other times, too—moments that still make me wonder how I processed everything as "not a big deal." As we grew, the gap in our four-year age difference got bigger. What started as "Go outside and play, and take your sister with you," turned into "You can go as long as you bring your sister." There were times I wondered if bringing me along was more about having someone to share the blame.

Whatever the reason, I became desensitized to the behaviors and began to believe they were simply part of childhood. Just life. Just normal.

Have you found yourself in a similar environment? Have you questioned why certain events were a part of your story?

I have learned not to question why things happened. It's more productive to look at events in your life and ask yourself what lesson they hold. Through my healing journey, I am beginning to understand that hurt people really do hurt people, and most often it isn't intentional. God has been revealing how some of my reactions—or overreactions—were born in those early moments when fear and fun blurred together.

I am learning to notice when my responses are larger than the situation in front of me and to ask God why I am reacting this way. Is there healing that still needs to be addressed? And the most significant part is that He is so tender with me, revealing bits and pieces as we go, loving me through the entire process.

Uncovering What Shaped You

1. Are there any areas in your childhood where, at the time, everything seemed normal, but looking back, you recognize they may have been unsafe or unhealthy?

2. Who are some people who helped shape your beliefs about safety, trust, or belonging? What beliefs that you held are you starting to recognize as untrue?

3. Are there any childhood patterns that are still showing up in your adult reactions? Some places I still need to dig deeper are

in the comments from the people I love most; the enemy tries to lure me back into agreeing with a spirit of rejection.

4. Ask God to reveal memories or places in your heart that still require healing. This will be a process, or at least it has been for me. Right when I think I'm all good, something comes up, and I wonder, "Where did that come from?" Then, it's back to the Lord in prayer, digging a little deeper with Him.

Here is a simple prayer you can say:

Dear Lord, I recognize that I overreacted in this situation (name it). I desire to be a representation of You and Your love in all circumstances. Please search my heart and reveal to me any places where I still need healing. Please help me understand the cause of this pain and replace any lies I believe or have believed with Your truth. In Jesus' name I pray. Amen.

Verses

Psalm 139:23–24 (NLT)

"Search me, O God, and know my heart; test me and know my anxious thoughts. Point out anything in me that offends you, and lead me along the path of everlasting life."

Ephesians 1:17 (NLT)

"I keep asking that the God of our Lord Jesus Christ, the glorious Father, may give you the Spirit of wisdom and revelation as you grow in your knowledge of him."

Awareness is often the first step toward healing, but it doesn't immediately fill the void. Long before I knew how to receive genuine love, I was already searching for it.

SIX

Looking for Love in All the Wrong Places

Love. It's something we all crave, yet so few of us truly know how to receive it. So, there I was, looking for love in all the wrong places.

Struggling with a spirit of rejection and parents who were so busy trying to build a business and keep their heads above water, I found myself longing for love and looking for it everywhere I shouldn't have been. Like many young girls, I thought if I could do enough, I'd finally feel sufficient.

It started with performance—striving to do my best at everything I did. A-honor roll, first chair clarinet, and often having the most aces in volleyball (which was quite an accomplishment if you know how vertically challenged I am). But that wasn't cutting it, because more often than not, my parents were too busy with their business commitments to attend my games and concerts.

Performance alone wasn't enough. I needed to look harder. This led to friendships—and friendships, paired with my previous desensitization, weren't a good combination. Those friendships led to boys. *Boys*...it would have been much more appropriate for them to hang out with my brother, not his little sister. Boys who had different things on their minds than I did. Boys I had no business spending time with.

You've probably witnessed this in your own life: people tend to do things at different ages and stages. For me, midway through my thirteenth year, this became an influence. Each step took me a little further from who I was—and a little closer to the world's version of love. I learned that the people I was spending time with, several years older than me, liked to get together on weekends and drink beer and smoke cigarettes. Remember, alcohol was around in many of my earliest memories, and I was desensitized to it. It had always been associated with people having a good time and laughing.

Do you recall any times in your life that now, looking back, you recognize not seeing a situation as you should have? For me, it was definitely alcohol. It started as just for fun, but it gets a grip on you. It's like I came to depend on it. The love that I so desperately wanted, I couldn't find with performance, friends, boys, or alcohol. I learned to hide behind my accomplishments. The partying was a great "cover" for someone just having a good time, and the alcohol had a dual purpose. It wasn't only a disguise, it was also my pain medication.

Looking back, my performance must have been a great cover because no one stepped in to intervene. Or perhaps, that was just the enemy's way to keep me in a place of rejection, where I wouldn't be able to grow into the divine calling on my life. What I didn't realize then was that the same enemy whispering lies about my worth was terrified of the purpose God placed inside me. Maybe my ability to hide behind performance shadowed the fact that I was playing on the enemy's playground. The truth is, the enemy will always use counterfeit comfort—busyness, attention, and accomplishment—to distract us from divine assignment. But God had already written redemption into my story.

Even in my wandering, God saw me. He knew the love I was searching for, and He was preparing someone who would reflect His steady grace.

By God's grace, the boy He knew I needed walked into my life when I least expected it.

There I was, working at the parts counter of my parents' marine and small-engine business one afternoon in early May. The door opened, quickly followed by a buzzing from the machine mounted alongside it, which signaled someone was coming in by breaking its infrared beam. I glanced over to see who was coming in, did a double-take, and may have been speechless, because I don't remember saying anything. I just stood there, trying to soak it all in—nonchalantly, of course. There stood a young man who made my heart race.

Nathan must have been who "they" were talking about when referring to a tall, dark, and handsome man. His mullet showcased the dark, coiled curls in the back. He had to have been a foot taller than me, and I can't believe someone didn't snag him to model that pair of Levi's he had on. I had to pull myself together. Nathan had gone into my parents' office to discuss the mechanic's job he had seen advertised in the local paper. It was only about 15 minutes or so when the door opened again, and Nathan was walking away as my dad told him to start the following weekend.

I'm sure my age of 17 shone through in all of my actions, having a coworker who made my heart skip a beat with every glimpse of him. It makes me giggle to recall all the times I thought I was being so discreet.

Looking back, my flirtatious style was anything but subtle. It was like a flashback to elementary school, passing notes in the classroom, face a little warm (and probably a little red, too), hoping the teacher wouldn't notice.

Do you like me? Check one:

Yes ☐ No ☐

The way the building was laid out meant customers would come through the front doors. They would bring in the piece of equipment that needed repair, describe the issue, and I would print out a repair order. A few times throughout the day, equipment and work orders would be brought to the mechanics in the back, to the work area. As you can imagine, I saw the need to get *all* the equipment to the mechanic as soon as possible, one at a time.

One particular memory is getting a weed trimmer back to Nathan. I, my stomach butterflies in tow, brought the trimmer to him and relayed what the customer was having trouble with. He asked for the work ticket, which I had forgotten, and I had to go back and get it.

Ingenious! I'm pretty sure that with every time *I forgot to grab the work ticket*, my tactics were revealed. In my naivety, I might as well have been carrying a neon sign around with me. Then, I had to try to decipher his thoughts when he would tell me to get back in the front, where I belonged.

Oh, to be young again... But beneath all the laughter and butterflies, something deeper was happening.

When we finally made it past the awkward flirting and started dating, I made myself completely available to him. I wanted to do whatever he did and go wherever he went. We had a great time fishing, hanging out with the boys, and doing the things guys do. I even overheard one of our friends call me "just one of the guys."

As the person seeking love while hiding behind performance, and with a primary love language of acts of service, I strove to be the best girlfriend I could be. I wanted to do whatever Nathan was doing or be wherever he was. At 18, I even bought property so I could live closer to him.

What I found was that, in the process of being who I thought Nathan wanted me to be—being deserving of his love—I lost out on learning who I was made to be. Don't get me wrong, I still love things like snowmobiling and everything about lake life (except the excessive bugs), but it wasn't until after we were married that I started learning new things I enjoy doing: flowers, preserving food, cooking, and traveling. Some even surprise me, like feeding the birds and seeing how unique they are both in physical characteristics and mannerisms. Like the beautiful blue jay, with the feathers on its back reminding me of a beautiful stained glass window, but it's such a messy eater! There are also the little chickadees that zoom into the feeder from out of nowhere, grab a sunflower, and zoom back to where they came from as quickly as they arrived. Or the excitement of seeing the birds that are just passing through, like the scarlet tanager, adorned in red, and the yellow-headed blackbird, which is not all that pretty but so unique. It shouldn't surprise me how much joy these things bring me, because that's how I was created; I just didn't take the time to learn sooner.

For so long, I tried to earn love through grades, performance, relationships, and even perfection. But the truth is, love isn't something we earn. It's something we receive. When I stopped chasing who I thought I needed to be and began to discover who God made me to be, peace and joy began to grow.

Take a few quiet minutes today and ask yourself:

- What am I doing to earn love or approval?
- Where have I lost touch with what genuinely brings me joy?
- What activities make me feel most like *me*—the person God handcrafted with purpose?

Write them down, and thank God for the small sparks of joy that remind you who He made you to be.

Verses

Psalm 139:14 (NLT)
"Thank you for making me so wonderfully complex! Your workmanship is marvelous—how well I know it."

Romans 8:28 (AMP)
"And we know [with great confidence] that God [who is deeply concerned about us] causes all things to work together [as a plan] for good for those who love God, to those who are called according to His plan and purpose."

I thought love would come through achievement or a relationship. Instead, God met me in a season I never planned and gave me a gift I didn't know my heart longed for.

SEVEN

The Gift I Never Knew I Wanted

Have you ever found yourself somewhere you weren't prepared for and didn't plan on, only to find out it was exactly where your heart secretly desired to be?

For me, that was motherhood.

Nathan has a beautiful niece who grew up knowing she wanted to be a mom. Me? I don't remember ever dreaming about having children. I wasn't against it—just indifferent. Playing with dolls was the closest I ever came to imagining motherhood. As a teenager, my goal was clear: become a successful businesswoman. Driven. Focused. Career-oriented.

But God, in His goodness and timing, knew what I needed long before I did.

It was my 24th birthday. Nathan had stopped over, and we were sitting in the living room by the fireplace; the slightest smell of wood smoke lingered in the air. It seemed like another ordinary day, that is, until he proposed to me. *Whirlwind*...that is how I describe the next five years. We were married just before I turned 25, and shortly after I turned 28, we had an infant and two toddlers.

Don't blink!

I often joke that I must have been created to be a mom because my pregnancies and deliveries were so uncomplicated. But the truth runs deeper: motherhood filled me in ways I never expected. It didn't just give me purpose, it softened places in me that had been hardened by performance, pressure, and striving for so long.

After Rachael arrived, I was grateful for my job, the flexibility they offered, the Family Medical Leave Act, and our moms who lived nearby. After maternity leave, I returned two days a week, leaving Rachael with my mom one day and with Nathan's mom the other. She was four months old before we needed daycare, and even then, Nathan and I carefully arranged our work schedules to minimize the time she was away from us.

Then, out of the blue, the company I worked for closed our location. No position. No notice. Just a severance package and workforce training.

I didn't see it then, but this was a door God was closing for me so He could open another.

I found myself at home, unsure where we'd go from there. Rachael was 13 months old, and I was five months pregnant. But God knew something I didn't: I would have never quit that job on my own. He knew the desires of my heart before I ever acknowledged them myself. Motherhood was the door He wanted wide open for me.

A year later, when a letter came from the new owners announcing job openings, I didn't even hesitate. I crumpled it up and threw it away. If they had known how deeply I loved my new "management position" they wouldn't have bothered. My heart was now firmly at home.

Ironically, my teenage vision of becoming a successful businesswoman was starting to take shape when I began my first management position at 26. Although it didn't look like anything I envisioned, it was the perfect next step for me. I was managing a young lady scurrying around in a diaper with a new hire on the way.

Unfortunately, the desires of our hearts don't always pay the bills.

Just under two years later, after Ethan, our youngest, was born, I started working as a waitress at a local supper club four nights a week. This transition allowed us to keep our children out of daycare and raise them ourselves. Even with some great options, we knew no one could love or care for our children as we would.

Nathan and I were able to shuffle schedules and keep the kids home with one of us most of the time. Working evenings, I only missed a few hours of the day when they weren't sleeping. I got dinner ready before I went to work, giving Nathan a little extra time for evening adventures.

By the time Ethan was in first grade, Nathan and I had been talking about whether or not it was time for me to get a "real" job. I was fully present in the mornings, but three days a week, shortly after they got off the bus, I left for work. After weighing the pros and cons, it didn't seem like the right option for us at the time because my hours away from home would increase while my income would decrease. We continued with Nathan working days primarily and me working nights, with a babysitter filling in the gaps when needed.

This is what our lives looked like for the next decade or so. I worked four nights a week, reserving Sundays for family time. Although I mostly saw Nathan in passing, I enjoyed being there when our children needed me and joining them on school field trips. I especially cherished our summers together.

And motherhood, something unplanned, unexpected, and undreamed of for me, became one of the greatest gifts God has given me.

Looking back, motherhood was one of the first and most obvious places where God was working at softening my heart, a heart that had been hardening for years. A heart reprogrammed to run on performance and approval was slowly being rewired by three of the most precious gifts God has entrusted to me.

Discovering the Doors God is Moving

- Look back at a door that closed.

Think back to a door that closed for you unexpectedly. Try to discover what you have now that you wouldn't have if that door hadn't closed. If you are struggling to remember, ask God to reveal it to you.

- Identify an open door you didn't expect.

Reflect on an opportunity, relationship, or season you never planned for but now recognize as a blessing. In what ways has God grown you through it?

- Pay attention to resistance.

Is there an area of your life where you keep pushing, but something keeps getting in your way? Ask God if that resistance is Him trying to guide you in a different direction.

- Ask God for clarity.

Pray, "Lord, help me see the doors You are opening and closing. I know Your ways are better than mine. Please help me remember that and trust You through the process."

Be sure to journal your thoughts.

- Surrender your timing.

God's timing is perfect. It's not always easy, but I find it helpful to tell God my desired outcome. I follow up with my desire for His will, not my own, and pray for guidance.

- Trust God with the unknown.

This isn't always easy, but it is key. One thing that has helped me is to have a reminder. On my office wall, I have a picture of a forest with train tracks that quickly disappear into the fog. It is a daily reminder for me to trust God, even when I can't see where He is leading me. Find a way to remind yourself too.

Verses

Ezekiel 36:26 (NLT)

"And I will give you a new heart, and I will put a new spirit in you. I will take out your stony, stubborn heart and give you a tender, responsive heart."

Proverbs 3:5–6 (NLT)

"Trust in the Lord with all your heart; do not depend on your own understanding. Seek his will in all you do, and he will show you which path to take."

My heart was fuller than it had ever been. What followed was a lesson I didn't know I needed—how to be filled without bursting, and how to let gratitude change everything.

EIGHT

Learning to Be Filled

The excitement I feel is almost uncontainable. Standing near the outside water spigot on the backside of the house, preparing for battle, with a green five-gallon bucket at my feet, a bag of empty balloons in my hand, a grin on my face, and a twinkle in my eye.

I crouch down and carefully spread the balloon's opening over the threaded faucet, then slowly turn the knob with one hand while supporting my balloon with the other. As the water slowly fills the balloon, I continually monitor the situation to ensure I have the perfect amount.

I didn't know it then, crouched by that faucet, but this moment would become the closest metaphor I've found for motherhood.

We all know that an underfilled water balloon is like giving the opposition free ammunition. It leaves your hand, flies through the air, only to bounce off the target and land harmlessly at their feet. You know it will be coming back at you.

Refocusing for a moment, it's back to filling the water balloons. Filling each one just right. Carefully removing it from the faucet, trying not to leave the balloon's collar stuck on the threads, and fighting to get the tiny neck tied.

It's not long before my mind wanders to the upcoming battle—imagining hiding places and letting the ambush play out in my mind.

The anticipation builds as I envision encountering my target, grabbing a balloon, and throwing it with all of my might.

In slow motion, the balloon travels through the air. *Impact.* The balloon bursts, water flies, and laughter is all that's heard. One more balloon to fill—just a little more water for extra drenching power.

And then, all of a sudden, capacity is exceeded with one final drop.

POP.

That's the closest I can come to describing how motherhood feels to me. Just like the water balloon, my heart feels filled with so much love that it's on the verge of bursting. Thankfully, my heart is far more pliable than those small water balloons.

Being a mom is one of the most precious gifts God has ever given me. Twenty-five years later, as I struggle to put words to the depth of my love and gratitude for our children, my eyes well with tears that can only be explained as being so full that, to keep my heart from bursting, some of it must overflow—spilling out as tears of joy.

That kind of overflowing love has taught me something unexpected. It has reshaped how I understand gratitude.

Have you ever found yourself in that place—so filled with gratitude that it almost bubbles over? It reminds me of a song we used to sing with the children in Sunday school about how "love comes bubbling through." If you've never experienced that kind of overflow, send me a message...because we need to talk.

That experience also made me realize something else: so much of life depends on mindset.

We've all seen it. Genuine gratitude isn't tied to material possessions. Some of the most grateful people I know don't have an abundance of things, while others seem unhappy no matter how much they have. Gratitude doesn't come from what we possess; it comes from within. Gratitude is a mindset—a choice.

I saw this play out clearly in a conversation Nathan and I had not long ago. We were talking about how our focus directly impacts what we notice.

What some people don't realize about living in Minnesota is that it can get hot in the summer. Nathan was on the phone with a friend who was really down in spirit. It was a hot summer day, and his central air conditioning had gone out. While waiting for the repair company, he drove around in his truck because at least the air conditioning there worked.

After the call, Nathan and I talked about how easy it is to focus on what's wrong: it's too hot, the AC is broken, I'm stuck driving around. That kind of focus creates a "bah humbug" attitude.

We also talked about how differently the day might have felt if his friend had focused instead on being grateful for having central air most days, a beautiful home, and a new truck to drive. It could have been a perfect day for an unplanned drive or a spontaneous trip to the beach.

Nothing about the situation changed—only the focus did. And that made all the difference.

That conversation reminded me of something Stephen Covey explains in *The 7 Habits of Highly Effective People*. He defines the word *responsibility* as our ability to choose how we respond in every situation.

This idea challenged me because it meant I couldn't blame my mood on circumstances anymore. The broken air conditioner was a perfect example. We can choose to be upset, or we can choose to be grateful. It isn't always easy, but it is possible when we're intentional.

I experienced this personally one summer day when I found myself in a blah mood for no particular reason. Nothing bad had happened, I just felt off. I decided to take a break from working in my office and head outside to water my flowers.

I grabbed my headphones, turned on one of my Christian playlists, and started singing along as I watered. Before long, I realized my mood had shifted entirely. What caused the change? Refocusing my attention to what brings me joy—flowers, music, praise, singing.

It's quite possible I brought others joy that day, too, especially if they happened to walk by while I was singing louder than I realized.

That moment made me aware of something powerful. I can refocus and change my mood by intentionally recalling what I'm grateful for or doing something that brings me joy. It helped me realize that my mood is my responsibility—not something happening to me, but something I can influence.

This realization is empowering. We can choose to sit in what brings us down, focusing on what we lack or what frustrates us in the moment. Or we can choose to remember our blessings. I've heard it said that negativity and joy can't occupy the same space at the same time.

And every time I choose gratitude, I'm reminded *it's always the better choice.*

So, have you ever felt so full of love, gratitude, or emotion that it almost felt overwhelming? Like one more drop might cause everything to spill over?

Motherhood has a way of stretching a woman's heart beyond what she thought it could hold. And yet it reveals a profound truth: overflow is often tied to our focus.

True gratitude doesn't just appear when our circumstances are perfect. It grows as we choose to notice what we have already been blessed with in every type of day: exciting, mundane, and hard ones alike.

As you reflect on this chapter, consider where your attention has been landing lately. Are you focused on what feels lacking or on what is quietly sustaining you?

Redirecting Your Focus

1. Notice Your Focus.

Pause and ask yourself, "What am I focusing on right now?" Learning to recognize where you are focusing your attention is the beginning of redirecting.

2. Name Three Gratitudes.

Make it a habit to write down three things you are grateful for each day—big ones and little ones alike. For me, sometimes it's the sunshine or the birds that come to visit the feeder.

3. Create a Mood-Shift Ritual.

Make a list of some of the activities that bring you joy—music, flowers, journaling, or going for a walk in nature, to name a few. Commit to doing one of these things when you feel off or overwhelmed.

4. Practice the Pause.

The next time a situation arises that you find frustrating, remember what Stephen Covey says about responsibility, and intentionally choose how you are going to respond in that situation. I pray you choose what brings peace.

5. Let Gratitude Spill Over

Share one thing you are grateful for, out loud, in a message, or in prayer. Overflow was never meant to stay contained.

Psalm 23:5 (NLT)
"You prepare a table before me in the presence of my enemies; you anoint my head with oil; my cup overflows."

James 1:2–3 (NLT)
"Dear brothers and sisters, when troubles of any kind come your way, consider it an opportunity for great joy. For you know that when your faith is tested, your endurance has a chance to grow."

I was learning how to live fully without bursting. What came next was discovering that fullness often precedes movement, and that God was quietly opening a door I hadn't been looking for.

NINE

The Door God Opened

It may have been one of the shortest phone calls I ever had with my mom, but what followed would impact my life forever.

It was a beautiful spring day in Minnesota on Thursday, May 31, 2018. The kids and I were on our way home from the Clay Target League High School Tournament. Conversations flowed easily—how the shooting went, what went well, what didn't, and how this year compared to the last.

The chatter was interrupted by an incoming call. It was my mom.

I remember the rest of that day as if it were yesterday. What she had to say was unusually vague, delivered through short, to-the-point questions.

What are you up to?
What time will you be home?
We have something to ask you.
Will Nathan be there?
Great, your dad and I will be over later.

The call ended almost as quickly as it began.

Have you ever had a conversation like this? It reminded me of when someone says, "Guess what?" followed immediately by, "Never mind."

What do you mean, never mind? I *do* mind. If you didn't want me to mind, you shouldn't have asked because now it's all I can think about.

For a short time after the call, my mind wandered, wondering what question could require an in-person visit. I even started to suspect it might have something to do with the latest MLM company my parents were involved in.

That thought likely stemmed from my long-standing struggle with people-pleasing—a continual longing for approval. It was the same thing that had led me to say yes the first two times my parents asked me to join their previous MLM adventures. I was young. I didn't really want to do it. And neither of those endeavors amounted to anything.

Even if they had asked, it wouldn't have mattered. It wasn't the right time for me.

They had started this most recent company three and a half years earlier, and I had been very clear: I wanted nothing to do with it. I was grateful the products had helped my dad so much, but as far as I was concerned, we were healthy. I didn't need those products, and I definitely didn't want to sell anything.

Overthinking it all ended quickly. After all, my parents hadn't pushed me to join or use the products in quite some time. They knew where I stood. I figured I'd find out what they wanted in a couple of hours.

With my mind temporarily freed, I enjoyed the rest of the hour-and-a-half drive home, listening to our three teenagers laugh and talk, music filling in the gaps.

We had just enough time to unload our gear and settle in when my parents pulled into the driveway. My memory might not be perfect, but it felt like the very first question after "hi" was when Nathan would be home.

Surface-level conversation filled the space until Nathan walked in. Then, came a quick hello—and straight to business.

There was a campaign. If they could get one more person to join them, they would earn a trip to Bali. And we were their last resort.

I told myself I'd be respectful. I said we would talk about it and let them know. But when I asked how long we had to decide, I can still picture my mom glancing at her watch and saying, "Eighteen minutes."

Her face said everything—*I'm sorry, please, hurry*—all wrapped up in sunshine, palm trees, and Bali beaches.

I felt incredibly put on the spot. How do you say no when you're standing between your parents and a dream vacation? They assured me they would help me earn the money back, but I didn't want hard feelings between Nathan and me.

Looking back, although we technically "talked" about the decision, there really wasn't time to discuss it. Something in my heart must have known that. So, I dove in, determined to earn the money back, and I did within two weeks.

And that is how my parents finagled me into their latest network marketing adventure. When people ask how I got started, I always say the same thing: *I came in kicking and screaming.*

It took me several years to realize it may have been the best business decision I ever made.

At the time, I was bartending four nights a week while managing life as a wife, mom, and household manager. Working nights had been a blessing when our kids were younger. But as they grew older, I started missing more and more of their lives.

Tuesday was the only night I could attend sporting events, so I had to choose which game to go to. I wasn't home after school to help with homework. And why didn't anyone warn me that teenagers become nocturnal? Eventually, I lost my mornings with them too.

When COVID hit in 2020, and Minnesota restaurants shut down, I found myself at home. For the first time in a long time, I had space to breathe, and clarity followed quickly.

When restaurants were allowed to reopen, I couldn't bring myself to go back. I vividly remember receiving the text message: my extended spring break was over, and I was expected back Thursday afternoon as usual. I cried.

When Nathan came home, I told him I was supposed to go back, that I didn't want to, and yes, I cried again. His response surprised me. "Then don't."

I gave my two weeks' notice, but I never made it back onto the schedule.

After enjoying the rest of the summer and into the fall, reality set in. I needed to contribute financially again. I was done working nights, but I still wasn't interested in getting a "real" job.

For the first time, I looked at my network marketing business differently. What I had treated as a hobby suddenly felt like an opportunity. Likely still driven by my desire for approval, I set my mind to business. And business took off.

By mid-2022, I realized that what had started as a favor to my parents had become a purpose. I was meeting incredible people, helping them get started with all-natural supplements, and hearing life-changing testimonies as their bodies began to function as they were created to.

That's when everything clicked. My passion for helping others came alive in those conversations—about health, hope, and possibility. My business grew quickly, and for the first time, the work felt deeply aligned. I was getting paid. I was earning incredible incentive trips. And most importantly, I was helping people transform their lives.

Looking back, I can clearly see how God was gently guiding me toward the door He was opening. He knew exactly how every piece needed to come together for me to step through it finally. Of course, He also knew I would eventually figure it out. It still amazes me how deeply God loves us—right where we are. His grace is abundant, and His patience is endless. Even in the midst of my stubbornness, He continued to guide me with gentleness and love, patiently waiting for me to notice His presence.

If God was so patient and intentional in guiding me through an open door I didn't initially recognize, I began to wonder where else He might be doing the same in my life...and where I may have been too distracted, hesitant, or afraid to notice.

Reflection Questions

1. Where has God opened a door that you didn't recognize at the time? How did it eventually shape or redirect your life?

2. Are there doors currently opening in your life that you've been hesitant to walk through? What fears, doubts, or assumptions might be holding you back?

3. **Have you ever mistaken God's patience for silence?** Are there ways God is gently guiding you right now?

4. Take a moment to pause, recognize God's presence, and ask Him to help you see the doors He is opening today.

God does not rush us through doors. We walk through them when we're ready to trust that He is already on the other side.

Verses

Isaiah 22:22 (NLT)
"I will give him the key to the house of David—the highest position in the royal court. When he opens doors, no one will be able to close them; when he closes doors, no one will be able to open them."

Proverbs 16:9 (ESV)
"The heart of man plans his way, but the Lord establishes his steps."

I had stepped through the door God opened, confident I was finally where I belonged. What I didn't yet understand was how quickly progress can stir resistance and how important it would be to keep climbing anyway.

TEN

Climbing Out of the Bucket

There we were, in the infinity pool overlooking the ocean on the northeastern shores of Mexico, when a woman I had just met pulled me aside and spoke words into me that I didn't yet know I would need to survive—or how soon I would need them.

This all-inclusive trip to Mexico was the first incentive trip I had earned for Nathan and me. We enjoyed being pampered and meeting people from all around the world. The most impactful part of the trip wasn't the wealth of knowledge from scientists and top leaders or the exquisite dinners and entertainment, but it was the time I spent with my new friends from Iceland. At one point, I was pulled aside for a tidbit of advice from one of the ladies.

To summarize what she had to say: She saw something very special in me and believed I had it in me to accomplish great things. With that, however, I would come across people who would try to drag me down, shut me up, or make me quit what I was building. I needed to be determined not to let that happen.

It reminded me of an analogy my dad told me decades earlier: when you have a bucket of crabs, you don't need to put a cover on it because if one tries to climb out to escape, the others will pull it back down. I believe my new friend basically told me that some people have a crabby mindset. Ha! She talked to Nathan as well, saying how some people would try to hold me back and keep me from excelling, and I would need him to be there for me, to encourage me, and keep me going. Who doesn't need a good cheerleader! She also commented that if he didn't, she would *find him...*

There's nothing like friends who have your back, right? Especially ones you just met! But I took her words to heart, and it's a good thing I did. I learned firsthand what she was warning me about much sooner than I imagined.

Not all resistance is obvious. Some of it comes quietly, from places you never expected.

I will never know a person's heart, but God does, and He gives us discernment. For good measure, He even throws in some good friends who have your back! With those tools, I began to recognize destructive behaviors more readily. It also came to my attention that some of my team members who were supposed to support me tried to tear me down behind my back.

Those moments can start to chip away at a person's self-worth and self-confidence. They are meant to pull you back down into the bucket where you "belong."

I hope you remember these words because I know you were created to have an impact on this world and the people who inhabit it. In the process, you are likely to find a few who are intimidated by your success, potential for success, or even the fact that you are trying to succeed. Those people will try to hold you back or get you to quit, but **you were created for greatness**, and you will never be alone because God is always with you.

As for me, shortly after that trip to Mexico, I quickly forgot about the poolside advice from my new feisty Iceland friend. I let others' negativity take over, and I almost gave up. In my stagnancy, I remember speakers saying, "You need a 'why that makes you cry,'" and, "Your dream isn't big enough," but I struggled with this too.

What I now realize is that we live in a world where we are told from a young age to get our heads out of the clouds, to quit daydreaming, or that dreaming won't pay the bills. Another thing I realized is that people were trying to motivate me with *their* dreams...a title, a monthly income, a sports car, etc. Their goals were impressive, but they didn't touch the deepest part of my heart. Because their dreams weren't my dreams, I couldn't relate, and I couldn't get excited for something that didn't align with my heart. For me, it wasn't about the income, and besides, I wanted a truck, not a sports car. I started to doubt whether I was meant to be in network marketing or even an entrepreneur at all. *Maybe I should go back to working at the bar.* I wanted to quit.

It was hard to deal with the things, both external and internal, coming against me. Thankfully, there was something inside, the still small voice, that wouldn't let me give up.

Not completely, anyway.

I found myself weighing the pros and cons of working from home versus bartending—the late nights and drama versus the flexibility and extra time with my family. I knew I didn't want to go back. So, I decided I needed to make some changes if I was going to regain momentum.

What followed was something I can only explain as God's grace.

Looking back now, I can see how intentionally God was rebuilding me—one step at a time.

Through what some would call coincidences, I ended up hearing a friend's podcast, joining an online Bible study, and being introduced to my first chronological Bible-in-a-year, which led me to read the Bible in its entirety for the first time in my life.

I also ended up joining a mastermind group with a couple of dozen top-earning women in different companies. This led to a great experience, where we learned, collaborated, and supported one another. There was no competition. We prayed together, prayed over each other, and built lifelong relationships.

His grace (the "coincidences") didn't stop there. During the mastermind, I was introduced to amazing people who led training sessions. I am still learning from some of these people through their podcasts. And there's the beautiful woman whom I was led to work with. She helped me through so much and equipped me with tools I needed not only to survive, but to thrive! She explained my feelings best when she said it's like she's holding one of my hands and God is holding the other. We were going through it together, and it was happening so fast! The connections didn't stop there. I feel so blessed to have the connections that keep unfolding, like a domino effect—blessings upon blessings upon blessings.

One of the greatest lessons I've learned is this: when your life feels like a bucket of crabs and you are finally climbing out, don't focus on the ones trying to pull you back down.

Look instead for the one longing for the courage to try.

Reach down and bring them with you.

You will find that you are blessed by this action just as much as they are.

Learning to Climb

Sometimes the resistance we face isn't loud or obvious. It doesn't always come from strangers or critics. It can come quietly—from people we expected to support us. Most often, it even comes from the voices we've allowed to take root in our own minds.

Take a moment to reflect on your own journey.

- Where in your life have you felt discouraged just as you were beginning to grow?
- Have there been moments when someone else's doubt, jealousy, or fear caused you to shrink back from what God was calling you to build?
- Are there voices you've been listening to that have kept you playing small, silent, or stuck?

Discernment is a gift from God. Not every opinion deserves space in your heart, and not every hand reaching for you is meant to lift you higher. Some are trying to pull you back into your comfort zone—even if it no longer fits who you are becoming.

As you reflect, ask God to reveal which voices are meant to sharpen you and which ones you are being invited to release. Climbing out of the bucket doesn't mean abandoning people; it means refusing to let fear or insecurity define your future.

And when you find yourself gaining clarity and courage, remember this: there is likely someone nearby watching you climb, longing for the bravery to try. As God strengthens you, ask Him who you might be called to encourage, invite, or lift alongside you.

Some days it might take all the strength you can muster to keep climbing. Just remember...

Somewhere, someone is waiting for you to climb out of that bucket and into your calling so they can be blessed through you.

Verses

Philippians 3:14 (NLT)
"I press on to reach the end of the race and receive the heavenly prize for which God, through Christ Jesus, is calling us."

Isaiah 30:21 (NLT)
"Your own ears will hear him. Right behind you, a voice will say, 'This is the way you should go,' whether to the right or to the left."

I had finally climbed out of the bucket. What I didn't realize was that the next part of my journey wouldn't be a mountaintop—but a valley.

ELEVEN

What the Valley Gave Me

Why didn't anyone tell me that I would climb out of the bucket and into the valley?

But if I had known ahead of time, I might have chosen to stay in the bucket. At least things were familiar there. But now that I was out? Well, just in case you don't know me well enough, I might have been just a little too stubborn to climb back in—back to the place where things were familiar.

The bucket may have been painful, but at least it was predictable. The valley was different. It was unfamiliar and uncomfortable...and if I'm being honest, it felt lonely at first.

Looking back, I am so grateful for that valley season.

The beginning of my growth started with what some would call coincidences, but I know better than that. One small moment led to another, and before I knew it, God had quietly begun rebuilding me from the inside out.

After wandering in the valley for a little while and having what one could almost call a pity party, I came across a social media post about a podcast Shan (one of my beautiful friends from the UK) was hosting. I was so excited for her, and I couldn't wait to listen.

I don't remember what the episode was about anymore, but I do remember she had Donna Johnson as a guest. At the end of the podcast, Donna mentioned the online weekly Bible study she hosted. I had some time on Wednesday mornings, so I decided to join.

Toward the end of October, Donna started talking about the Daily Bible she reads and encouraged others to join her in reading it. That was the first time I had ever set out to read the entire Bible in one year.

I wasn't new to reading the Bible. By this point in my life, I had been teaching Sunday school for close to 20 years. But this time, I experienced the Bible in a way I never had before. There was a depth I hadn't encountered, and God was speaking into me through His Word.

I really enjoyed reading the Bible chronologically. It helped bring the different accounts to life. I was excited to see what was coming next; even the stories I had heard since childhood suddenly spoke to me differently.

I am now in the early stages of my third year of reading through the Bible. And I've come to realize that each year is a new experience because God shows me something different every time. I know He is speaking to me and revealing new things through His Word again and again.

Around that same time, I joined a mastermind group with Sarah Robbins for Christian women leaders in the network marketing industry. Looking back, I see how intentional God was being. He wasn't only restoring my faith. He was also restoring the people around me, bringing in friendships, mentors, and a community that strengthened me in ways I didn't even know I needed.

The community taught me so much about the people I surround myself with. I had never encountered a group of successful women who were eager to help, collaborate, and cheer one another on. Some of the friendships I made there will last a lifetime.

Each month, as I mentioned, we also had guest speakers come in to train us on various topics that benefited us collectively, deepening my knowledge. One thing I want to mention is that although all the guest speakers were very knowledgeable, I didn't resonate with each of them equally, and that's okay. It doesn't mean one was better than another. It just means one was better for me in the season I was in. Sometimes, I believe, those connections are a little nudge from God toward the direction He wants us to go.

Over those two years, the person I resonated with most was the wife of an exorcist. I can say *exorcist* because she wrote a book with that in the title. It still brings a smile to my face—and a couple of giggles too—as I picture her reading this sentence!

As I try to find the words to describe everything Cathy Greer did for me, the best I can come up with is this: she equipped me.

Cathy not only helped me work through my past, but also helped me experience the Father's love and recognize His presence in my everyday life. She helped me realize how many of the choices I had made, especially the ones rooted in people-pleasing, were driven by an emptiness deep inside me.

The most impactful, life-changing realization was this: The missing piece of my puzzle couldn't be filled by the people or things of this world. A relationship with my Heavenly Father was what it would take to fill the void.

Knowing who He calls me, learning to see myself as He does, and starting to dream with Him is allowing me to become the person He created me to be.

And just when I thought God had already surrounded me with more support than I deserved, Cathy introduced me to another beautiful woman—someone who would help me find my voice and encourage me to write this book.

Her name is Melissa Lea Hughes...or as I like to call her, Melissa the Miner, because she is so good at digging down and getting to the goods I didn't know how to find on my own. She encourages me to dream with God, aligning my desires with the calling on my life.

Melissa is my encourager. She's all about seeking God and following it up with radical action. I love her phrase, "It's sweaty armpit time," reminding me that even though it's scary, and I'm starting to perspire, you grab the deodorant and go anyway.

She is a beautiful representation of a princess—the King's daughter.

Looking back, that valley season was a whirlwind. I know some might say it was all just a bunch of coincidences, but I know better.

As humans, it seems most of us dread the valley seasons and would do almost anything to steer clear of them. We prefer the mountaintops, which are beautiful and fun. And I would have agreed with you...until now.

Because after walking through the valley with awareness—and with a support network that God put in place at just the right time—I wouldn't trade it for anything. There was growth in the valley I wouldn't have received on the mountaintop.

And even greater than the growth was this: God met me in that valley. He used that season to draw me closer to Him. It was in the darkness of the valley where His light shone the brightest...and I'm not sure I would have had the eyes to see it anywhere else.

When I entered that valley season, there stood a frightened, self-conscious, broken little girl in a woman's body. But the healing and growth I received on my journey through the valley changed everything.

Because now I know this: the valley doesn't destroy me, it develops me. I won't run from it. I won't numb it. I won't let it define me. I will walk through it with God, eyes up and heart anchored, because I know I will come out stronger and closer to my Father on the other side.

What the Valley Gave Me

The valley seasons are rarely dramatic. They are often quiet, stretching, and deeply personal. They slow us down and gently reveal what we have been carrying and what we were never meant to carry alone. It is often in these hidden places that God does His most intimate work.

Take a moment to reflect on your own journey.

1. Where in your life have you walked through a valley you didn't choose?
2. What emotions surfaced in that season that you had been avoiding or silencing?
3. What did the valley strip away—roles, expectations, or identities you were clinging to?

4. Who did God place beside you in that season to support, guide, or encourage you?

5. Looking back, what did God give you in the valley that you might not have received anywhere else?

6. How has that season shaped the way you trust God today?

The valley does not mean you are behind, forgotten, or failing. It is often the place where God is doing His most intentional work—forming your faith, strengthening your trust, and reminding you who you are in Him. What feels like loss may actually be preparation for what lies ahead. So, enjoy the journey with Him. It will be worth every step you take.

Verses

Deuteronomy 31:6 (ESV)
"Be strong and courageous. Do not fear or be in dread of them, for it is the LORD your God who goes with you. He will not leave you or forsake you."

Isaiah 54:2–3 (NKJV)
"Enlarge the place of your tent, and let them stretch out the curtains of your dwellings; do not spare; lengthen your cords, and strengthen your stakes. For you shall expand to the right and to the left, and your descendants will inherit the nations, and make the desolate cities inhabited."

Healing prepares the heart, but identity requires stillness. After the valley, I found myself asking a deeper question—not what I should do next, but who God says I am.

TWELVE

Who He Calls Me

I'm not sure how to explain the feelings I had when I realized that I had spent half of my life without knowing who God calls me. Or, for that matter, that He even has a name just for me.

I didn't know I was missing it—until the moment I found it.

The first time someone told me about Jamie Winship's book *Living Fearless*, I think I had it in my Amazon cart within a few hours. I don't recall exactly how it was described to me, but I remember feeling excited and starting it right away. I quickly realized it was the right book for me at precisely the right time.

I'm not sure if you've been there, but I can't count the number of times I've picked up a book and struggled to get through the first few chapters, only to place it back on the bookshelf. Some books resonate deeply with me, and some don't. I've learned that sometimes a book isn't a match, or perhaps it's just not the right fit for the season I'm in. Often, I can return to a previously set-aside book and find that I enjoy it the second or third attempt at reading it.

When I started reading Jamie's book, he recommended reading it straight through and getting away somewhere alone, with limited distractions. Within a couple of hours, I found myself browsing VRBO listings and planning a one-day retreat within driving distance of my home. I knew what I was supposed to do, but I couldn't wait until the retreat arrived. I read the first 50 pages while I waited—just until the book's depth truly began.

Looking back, I know God gave me guidance in choosing the place, because it was perfect—right down to the sketchy cell phone signal, just in case my willpower wasn't strong enough to stay off my phone.

It was late spring in 2023. The sun was shining as I drove down winding roads, filled with anticipation for what lay ahead. Following the GPS, I turned onto a gravel road and went for a couple of miles. I actually passed the driveway and had to turn around. As I pulled in, it wasn't at all what I had expected. I'm not sure what I *had* expected, but this wasn't it.

Tall pines surrounded the area, leaving only thin grass beneath them. I remember feeling slightly disappointed, because I love a lawn full of thick, plush grass soaking up the sun. There wasn't much lawn at all, and with all the trees, not much sun either. The driveway ran alongside the house, and less than 50 feet away was a dock I would later find myself standing on.

I crossed the gravel road to check in and met a lovely couple. The husband even gave me a tour of the loft he had built for his homing pigeons, which delighted me, since we've had homing pigeons for over 20 years and I had only seen how a couple of others had theirs set up. After the tour, he showed me to my tiny home for the night.

I unpacked, grabbed my book, notebook, pen, and water bottle, and headed outside to the patio table overlooking the lake.

I will never forget what happened over the next few hours.

Sitting there on that warm afternoon in late May, shaded by towering pines, I felt an overwhelming sense of peace. To my left was the house. To my right, a wooded incline where a chipmunk kept catching my attention as he darted through the trees. Straight ahead was the lake with a periodic fish jumping out of the water, causing ripples to travel across the otherwise glass-like surface.

I opened my book and picked up where I had left off.

After reading the prayer out loud, I asked the first question:

God, what is the most crucial thing You want to say to me right now?

And His response was...nothing. Silence.

No matter how intently I listened, all I heard was the soft rustling of the chipmunk nearby.

I refused to give up. I'm not sure if He knows how stubborn I can be—well, of course, He does—but I kept listening and waiting. Looking back, I believe that was the point. The silence made me still and pay closer attention.

Here is what I journaled after that very first unanswered question:

You are with me.
I hear You in the breeze moving through the trees.
I hear You in the birds singing their songs of praise.
I feel You in the tightness of my chest.

You are with me.

The wind is picking up as You draw nearer.
Every time I ask the question, the wind moves more.

I can feel Your presence and "see" the Spirit moving through the woods around me.

You are with me.

And that was the most important thing He wanted me to know in that moment—not just to *know* it, but to *experience* it. If you know, you know. Experiencing God's presence and love is powerful and life-changing. Learning how He communicates with *you* is essential.

So, back to the patio.

After that moment, I continued through the questions Jamie encouraged me to ask God, writing down the answers that came to mind. They were powerful. Enlightening. Often just one word or phrase. But as I sat with each one, a deeper understanding unfolded.

What did I take from that section of the book? That God knows my deepest thoughts and feelings. He knows exactly where I struggle and wants to help me. More than that, He wanted me to know I am loved, forgiven, and more than enough. I am not defined by my past, my sins, or my failures. He already took care of that. Why would I allow those things to determine my self-perception when God's view of me is entirely different?

In big letters across my journal, I wrote:

LORD—teach me to live in my true identity.
Finally, I reached the question.
What do you call me, Lord?
Healer.

I was disappointed. It felt so plain. Almost boring. I questioned Him, much like Abraham questioned God about Sodom and Gomorrah's upcoming destruction and how many righteous people needed to be living there for Him to spare the towns. Surely there was more. Jamie's son was called *Skateboarder for Christ,* which sounded far more exciting.

What had I expected?
Beautiful Princess Warrior?
Courageous Princess Peacemaker?

Eventually, after some honest discussion, the title expanded.

Healer of the Brokenhearted.

I began to cry. Sitting there at the little rental, immersed in God's presence, having an internal conversation with my Father, I was utterly overcome by emotion and love.

For the first time, I understood my God-given purpose. Even more than that, I understood how the things I had walked through could be used to help others—to help heal broken hearts. Because this is who He calls me.

Healer of the Brokenhearted.

Although, I may need to modify my title and work "princess" in there somewhere. After all, I am a daughter of the King.

That overnight trip was one of the most life-changing experiences of my life. I now know my identity in Christ—who He calls me and why I'm here. We can read all we want about being created on purpose and for a purpose, but the strength comes when we ask God what that purpose is.

This is when we begin to walk in our God-given authority, fully confident in who we are in Him.

Who Does God Call You?

Be still before seeking answers. Sometimes the most important thing God wants us to know isn't something we *do* but something we *receive*—His presence, His voice, His truth.

Spend a few quiet moments with God before responding to the questions below.

1. What names am I calling myself?

Ask God to bring to mind any names, roles, or identities you've accepted that did not come from Him. These may be words spoken over you by others or ones you quietly spoke over yourself.

2. Where am I striving instead of listening to You?

Where in your life have you tried to define who you are through achievement, roles, approval, or performance instead of listening to what God calls you?

3. Remember moments when you have been in His presence.

When have you felt intensely aware of God's nearness, even without words? What did that moment feel like? What did it awaken in you?

4. Ask the question!

Take a deep breath. With an open heart, ask,

"God, who do You call me?"

Write down the first word, phrase, or image that comes to mind. Don't rush past it. Sit with it. Ask Him what He wants you to understand about it.

God created you for a purpose. He knew you before the beginning of time, and He loves you more than you could ever imagine. He waits for you—to spend time with Him in stillness, in His presence—where He can heal your broken heart and fill you with His love.

Verses

Psalm 138:8 (NLT)

"The LORD will work out his plans for my life—for your faithful love, O LORD, endures forever. Don't abandon me, for you made me."

Isaiah 45:3 (NASB)

"I will give you the treasures of darkness and hidden wealth of secret places, so that you may know that I, the Lord, who call you by your name, am the God of Israel."

When your identity becomes clear, your discernment sharpens. I started noticing how the people around me were either reinforcing who God says I am or subtly challenging it.

THIRTEEN

The Company We Keep

As an adult, do you ever catch your parents' voices echoing in your thoughts? It's often in a tone you're convinced they never actually used, yet it's precisely how it registered in your mind as a teenager.

I'm sure you have heard these exact words coming from the mouths of your parents: "You are who you hang out with," or "Is that what you want your life to look like when you grow up?" I can still imagine myself rolling my eyes as these words are said in an exaggerated tone in my mind. However, as I grow and age, I have come to see more clearly the truth behind those words, especially regarding the influence of the people around us. I have not only recognized it in myself but have also witnessed it in others.

I clearly remember joking around with Nathan one time when I told him, "You're going to have to take a break from hanging out with Henry for a little while because you are starting to talk like him." (His friend I was talking about isn't really named Henry, but I wanted to protect the guilty here.) Nothing bad was meant by the statement, of course, but it is a clear example of how we become the average of the handful of people we spend the most time with.

Raising children, if you pay attention, you can pick it out as well. Vocabulary is only one of the things that change as their friends do. Clothing, activities, and attitudes can all change too. And while it's easy to notice these shifts in children, it's harder—but just as important—to recognize them in ourselves.

For me, it's not only in the words I use, but more importantly, in my attitude. And if you tell Nathan I said that, I'll deny it, of course.

Let me give you an example of how subtle this can be. Imagine with me a beautiful spring morning, and birds are singing away as they gather their nesting supplies. The grass is turning green, buds are beginning to show signs of life on the trees, and the air carries a crisp, fresh scent. You inhale a deep breath to take it all in. As you round a bend in the road that follows the shape of the lake, you meet Shelly, who recently moved into the area just down the street. You knew from that moment on that you had found a new friend. Your daily walks are just the beginning of what you do together. Shopping trips, kayaking, and flower gardening quickly join the list. Spring turns into summer, which turns into fall.

Out of the blue one morning, the realization hits you that you haven't felt the same optimistic, happy self. You begin to pay attention to the influences in your life, both internal and external. The next day, when you meet Shelly for your daily walk, you notice your mood has declined slightly. As you try to find the cause, you realize Shelly is complaining about her job and a co-worker. Over the next several weeks, you begin to notice a pattern of complaining. You start to get sucked down into the same pattern of complaining too. Instead of looking at the bright side of situations, you begin to focus on the negative, a habit that spirals out of control. Eventually, you decide to take a break from spending so much time with Shelly. You start to notice that you are becoming more optimistic again. You are getting back to being your joyful self. Nothing dramatic had happened, but something significant had quietly shifted.

The most dangerous influences aren't always loud or malicious. Often, they're quiet companions we never thought to question.

I can see stories like that throughout life, both in my own and in others'. That warning I rolled my eyes at decades ago played out right in front of my eyes, over and over again.

Do you recognize similarities to events in your past or present?

So...now what?

Run! As fast as you can, run!

If only it were that simple. Sometimes, yes, it can be, but most often it's not. We actually have to deal with it, but I promise you it will be worth it.

One of the most helpful ways I learned to think about this came through a simple framework. I remember Cathy telling me how Jesus had His 3, 12, and 72. She was trying to point out to me the different levels of friendships we have. Our "72" are the people who are more than mere acquaintances. We may not see them often, but when we do, we can carry on a conversation as if we were just together yesterday! Our "12" are the people we live life with, doing things and talking with regularly. Then, there's our "3." These are our besties—the ones who know everything about us. Those we call first when there's excellent news to share or we need a shoulder to cry on. The ones who will walk through the trenches with us and carry us when we don't have the strength to continue. Our inner circle.

But influence doesn't stop with relationships. It's not only who we spend our time with that shapes us, but it's also what we watch, listen to, and read—all of which strongly influence who we become.

To grow, we need to hear and read things that expand our knowledge and skill set. If we only ever read books at a 3rd-grade level, we will struggle to read anything beyond that. Watching shows filled with violence, swearing, and immorality desensitizes us to the sin. What we repeatedly consume trains our nervous system, our thoughts, and eventually our beliefs about what is normal.

Plainly put, you spend a lot of time around angry people, and you'll tend to become angrier. Or when you are in environments where people curse a lot...you get it. Both our surroundings and who we surround ourselves with are critical, even as adults.

Me? I began to become aware of who I surround myself with and what I take away from them. I moved relationships from my 3 or 12 out to my 72, deciding I didn't want their influences shaping who I was becoming. It's not going to be easy. We need to be intentional about what influences we allow to shape our future. And people will move around within your circles for many different reasons because we go through seasons in life and grow at various paces.

It wasn't until I started surrounding myself with Christian women who deserved to be in my inner circle that I realized how imperative it was. Inside those circles, we all benefited. Not because we were perfect, but because we were intentional about pointing each other back to God. Together, we prayed and praised, laughed and cried, supported and cheered each other on. We built each other up, and each one of us grew in some way through our time together. These are the kind of people you want to surround yourself with—women who pour into you and pray for your success. Women who speak well of you, no matter who is listening, and challenge you to grow into the person you were created to be.

As you continue on your journey in this life, I encourage you to pay close attention to who is in your innermost circles. And to make it a habit to review and transition as needed. Remember, as you grow, you are going to outgrow some relationships and grow into others, and that's okay. Just because you outgrow someone doesn't mean you can't be friends anymore; they just have a different role in this season.

I was listening to a podcast today, and they briefly touched on the "iron sharpens iron" principle. Ideally, the relationships that support the most substantial personal growth are having one person ahead of you, leading and guiding you; someone alongside you, growing with you; and someone a little further behind whom you are leading. They concluded that in a circle like that, you would be the "sharpest."

Who Is Your *Company*

Influence is rarely evident in the moment. More often than not, it slowly shapes our thoughts, attitudes, and beliefs. Becoming aware of who we allow access to us is an act of wisdom, not judgment.

Take some time to reflect on the following:

- Notice Your Circles.

Who is in your inner circles now, the people you talk with most, confide in, and do life alongside?

How do you feel after spending time with them—encouraged, peaceful, drained, or unsettled?

- Pay Attention to Patterns.

Are there relationships or environments that consistently pull you toward negativity, comparison, gossip, or discouragement?

Are there people who gently challenge you, pray with you, and call you higher—even when it's uncomfortable?

- Consider What Shapes You.

What voices regularly influence you through what you watch, listen to, or read?

Do those inputs align with the person you are becoming and the life God is calling you to live?

- Choosing with Intention

Growth often requires adjustment. Not every relationship needs to be removed, but some may need to be repositioned for this season.

Ask yourself:

- Is there anyone who may need to move from a closer circle to a more distant one?

- Is there someone God may be inviting you to draw closer to?

- Are there habits or influences you need to limit to protect your peace and spiritual growth?

Bring these questions to God in prayer. Ask Him for discernment, grace, and courage to make changes with love and wisdom.

Remember, outgrowing relationships doesn't mean you are rejecting the person. It simply means honoring the season you are in and the direction you are growing.

Verses

Proverbs 13:20 (NASB)
"He who walks with wise people will be wise, But a companion of fools will suffer harm."

1 Thessalonians 5:11 (NLT)
"Therefore, encourage one another and build each other up, just as you are already doing."

With my identity anchored and my circle intentional, a quiet question surfaced—one I had never asked before. I wasn't questioning whether God was real. I was beginning to realize I hadn't consistently recognized how near He was.

FOURTEEN

Loved in the Stillness

I didn't know that the most profound understanding of God's love would come to me in stillness. Looking back, I can see how God didn't just bring Cathy into my life to help me change my thoughts; He brought her to help me change how I understood His heart.

Love was a big one.

Jesus loves me, this I know,
For the Bible tells me so.

Although we are taught those words from a young age, there is still the problem of understanding what such love is. We compare that love to the only love we've known: The love we receive from our families and friends. From our fellow sinners, who learned how to love from other fellow sinners. We don't know how to love unconditionally. Our sinful nature keeps us from doing so.

Since this is the only love we know, Jesus' love is defined in our hearts in the same manner. That is precisely where Cathy found me.

God loves me. And how did God love me? Exactly how I learned about love in all of my brokenness.

God loved me when I behaved. God loved me when I performed well and when I was on my best behavior. God loved me when I gave Him what He wanted.

What about when that moment passed or when I didn't meet the expectations?

Then, I was scolded, punished, ignored, unfriended, etc., etc., etc. Why? Because those are the things we experience sometimes from the fallen nature of the people we love. People who are doing their best to love us from their own brokenness.

Conditional love is what we know and what we give. But the love that Jesus loves me (and you) with is so much more. We know what unconditional love is in theory, but it is hard for us to grasp.

As a parent, I love my children unconditionally.

BUT...

I always fall short of showing them love unconditionally because I am a sinner. I get hurt. I get offended. I sometimes even direct my frustrations at them, even when they are in no way involved. Not that I mean to, but I think subconsciously, I know they will forgive me. And that is how my children learned about love. Without realizing it, this is how my understanding of love—and God—had been shaped.

This is hard to admit, and it is definitely not how I want to show my love to anyone, much less to those I love most. But it is something to recognize when we look at the big picture of what goes into our understanding of love—the love we use to define how Jesus loves us.

As painful as the realization was, it helped me understand something even more profound: this was the lens through which I viewed God.

Cathy said something that really hit home (and continues to come to mind periodically): You know God loves you, right? But do you know that He likes you too?

Ouch. That was painful, yet it ignited something deep within me—a clashing blend of emotions. The question itself was unsettling; love felt distant and abstract, but liking felt intensely personal.

I understand the love me part. You can love everyone, and we are called to do so. But *like* me? To like a person, you need to know them. To know someone, you have to have some relationship with them.

I had recognized God's love for me as *agape love*, which is so true. It is the sacrificial love of God that sent Jesus to the cross for my sins, for all of our sins. I am a sinner, I can't save myself, so Jesus' death on the cross was an act of sacrificing His life in place of mine. He died for my sins so I didn't have to. His blood washed away my sins.

He washed away my sins, making me righteous in God's eyes and deserving of eternal life, not by works that I have done, but by the grace of God.

The part of God's agape love that was tainted for me was my understanding of it. I knew God loved me, but I also knew I didn't deserve it.

My problem? I knew I wasn't worthy of His love. In my mind, it was like this: Jesus died on the cross. He loved me because He *had to*. I know it sounds childish, but that is where I was at. And then...

God used Cathy to bring me a deeper understanding of love and a different lens through which to view it. What I didn't realize was that my understanding of God's love was incomplete. It turns out agape love isn't the only kind of love God has for us. Phileo love was the key I was missing.

While agape love is the kind of love that is of the will, a love you choose to give, phileo love is more experiential. I have read that the best definition of this kind of love is "to cherish."

To cherish!

Cathy challenged me to go through the book of John in the Bible and underline Father every time it appears in the chapter. "Go through the verse and look at the type of love that is shown," she advised. She also directed me to a book about God's love for me. Little did I know what would happen.

Right there, in my living room, God's love broke through the hardness of my heart.

Imagine with me for a moment. It's a spring morning with a fog so heavy that it's hard to see much farther than a few steps ahead. You feel drawn down a trail, even though you can't see well and are unsure of what lies ahead. It's so unfamiliar, but you can't ignore the feeling of being drawn forward. It's as though your feet take the next steps on their own. As you continue, anticipation grows. And the moment you get there, it's so much more than you could have imagined.

It was as though I took that journey without ever leaving my chair. As God's love seeped through, it was as though I was on this journey to the depths of my soul, uncertain of what I would find when I got there.

What did I find?

Jesus, squatting down with arms wide open, calling me to come to Him, wrapping His arms around me, and telling me He had been waiting for me. He had been waiting for me to notice Him there.

He wanted so much more for me—more than knowing He chose to die on the cross for me because He loves me. He also wanted me to know that He cherishes me. He delights in me. He wants an intimate relationship with me.

And that changed everything.

God likes me because He wants to! I learned I was enough, despite all my shortcomings. My past mistakes didn't change this fact and neither would my future ones. He wants me to include Him in my day-to-day life, choices, feelings, and everything else that goes along with it.

Jesus loves me. He likes me. Now, it was time to learn to be still so we can have two-way communication. Once I understood that kind of love, the question became *how do I stay connected to it?*

Be still.

Those two words are so simple yet so difficult. We live in a world that has become anything but still. Six months or so after I quit working my bartending job, I remember packing so much into my days that I wasn't sure how I ever had time to work so many hours.

Don't get me wrong. It is good to work and be productive. The problem is, when we fill our schedules to the brim, we don't have time to be still with our Lord and Savior.

For me, being still took practice. If I am being sincere, it still does at times. And the enemy is always lurking in the shadows, trying to convince us we don't have time for that. *You are running late today. You overbooked your schedule, and something has to go.* Don't fall for his tricks. The enemy knows full well that if you spend time intimately with God, it will draw you further from the darkness into the light.

As you learn to sit with God in stillness, talk with Him like you would your best friend. Share your day, your concerns, your hopes, and your dreams. I struggled with this at the beginning because He already knew it all. Why did I need to tell Him?

I'm learning that, although He already knows all things, the act of telling Him changes us. Drawing closer to Him, we grow our relationship and build more trust.

I don't have my scheduling all figured out yet, but I am working on it. What I do know is that I like to take time first thing in the morning to be still with God. Leaving my phone on Do Not Disturb until I am finished with my time with my Savior in the morning helps me stay focused. It doesn't always work, but it definitely helps. Various habits help me connect with Him and receive His guidance. I read the Bible, pray, journal, listen to worship music, read devotionals, and take various studies to deepen my understanding. This time is a must for me, and would be extremely beneficial for you too. Growing deeper in intimacy with our Creator is one thing where the reward is far greater than the cost. Especially because as you grow in wisdom, you will find yourself eager to go deeper with God.

Being Loved in the Stillness

For many of us, the most challenging part of our relationship with God isn't believing He loves us, it is learning how to receive His love without striving for it. We are so familiar with performance, productivity, and proving our worth that stillness can feel uncomfortable, even unproductive. Yet, it is often in the quiet moments when we stop trying to earn His approval that God reminds us of who we already are.

Stillness is not about doing nothing. It is about choosing presence over performance. We allow God to meet us exactly where we are, without hiding ourselves, our expectations, or effort. When we come before Him in stillness, simply desiring to be with Him, we make space to experience not only His love for us, but His delight in us. Yes, He delights in you.

If you're willing, try adding the following to your morning routine.

- With a journal and pen, find a quiet, distraction-free space to sit with God.
- Imagine yourself sandwiched between God on your left and Jesus on your right.
- Take a few deep, relaxing breaths.
- Tell God, "I am here."
- Sit in His presence—fully known and fully loved.

It might feel awkward at first, and that's okay. You're learning something new. If your mind begins to wander, gently refocus on Him. If something keeps pulling at your attention, write it down and return to His presence.

Afterward, I like to journal about whatever I am led to—plans, goals, dreams, fears—bringing everything before the One who loved me long before I was ever born.

Verses

Psalm 145:18 (ESV)
"The Lord is near to all who call on him, to all who call on him in truth."

Romans 15:13 (NLT)
"I pray that God, the source of hope, will fill you with joy and peace because you trust in him. Then you will overflow with confident hope through the power of the Holy Spirit."

Once I learned to be still with God, I realized His love wasn't meant to end in comfort. It was there, in the stillness, that I understood He wasn't only healing my past, He was inviting me to dream with Him about what lies ahead. And just like that, it was as though I was a little girl again, using my imagination and learning how to dream with God.

FIFTEEN

Learning to Dream Again

I didn't know how to answer when someone asked me what my dreams were. By that point, I had begun recognizing God's presence in my life in ways I never had before, but dreaming still felt unfamiliar.

When asked, "I don't know" was often my reply. And the truth is, that answer surprised me.

We have all heard statements over the years such as, "Dreaming doesn't pay the bills," and "Get your head out of the clouds." But when I became more intentional about who I surround myself with, I started being asked a different kind of question—one I wasn't prepared for.

Who has time to dream? I definitely didn't; I was too busy living. Working, along with all of the responsibilities of being a wife and mom seemed to take up every spare moment.

I'm not really sure when I quit dreaming. Honestly, I'm not sure I ever started. I remember using my imagination as a young girl. But actual dreaming? I don't really remember that. I'm realizing—maybe even in this moment—that I was more prone to set my mind on accomplishing something than actually dreaming about what it would be like when I did.

Looking back now, I can see that I learned early how to set my mind to something but not how to dream about it. For example, I recall having a credit card at 18. I remember the stress of being unable to pay the bill in full and carrying part of the balance. I did get it paid off, of course, but I hadn't learned the full lesson. When I accumulated another $1,500 balance and paid it off at 21, I set my mind not to put anything on my credit card that I couldn't pay off in full at the end of the month. That discipline, along with the blessing of Nathan and me always having incomes, has allowed us to avoid paying any credit card interest for almost three decades. Over the years, this attention to loan costs has carried over into an aggressive approach to paying off everything we have purchased with borrowed money.

I am making the connection between setting my mind to something and dreaming, but let's be real. There's also a connection between school playgrounds and amusement parks. You go to both for enjoyment; amusement parks are on another level.

Playgrounds represent what we set our minds to—our disciplines, basically. We pay our bills on time and pay them off as quickly as possible. We exercise frequently, read daily, and keep our houses clean. Those mindsets help us achieve our goals, but they can be mundane and probably don't bring us much joy in the moment.

Amusement parks are filled with anticipation, excitement, and expectancy. It's as though I become childlike in the moment. The feelings we get when we are dreaming aren't ones we usually have daily in the process of adulting.

But honestly...it's hard to dream! Especially when you've trained yourself to be responsible instead of hopeful. Somewhere along the way, I must have either put my right to dream on a shelf, forgotten how to dream, or never even learned how.

When I first decided to give dreaming a try, I felt an internal struggle: the inner child urging me to go to the amusement park and the adult in me saying, "I don't have time for that anymore." It was as though I had a reality check going on, and I wouldn't allow myself to truly dream. *Nonsense*, I would think and then carry on with my day in "real life." And without realizing it, I kept choosing survival over imagination.

What I didn't realize was that those beliefs were only making it more challenging. That mindset, paired with people trying to encourage me to borrow *their* dreams, was a losing combination. Another thing I didn't understand yet was that not all dreams are transferable.

Have you ever had someone try to encourage you with their dreams? Unless their dreams align with yours, it does no good. You can tell me to stand in front of this fancy sports car, take a picture with it, and put it on my dream board. But you might need to consider this: if I don't like fancy sports cars, putting a picture of one where I can see it daily isn't going to help me dream at all.

Instead of trying to inspire someone by simply sharing your own dreams, it's more effective to help them learn to dream again. First, invest time in getting to know them. Ask questions about their likes and dislikes to better understand their heart's desires.

Another barrier to dreaming surprised me even more: dreaming felt selfish.

Was it a poverty mindset? Or maybe just overflowing gratitude combined with the knowledge that the majority of the world's population would be thrilled with the many things I have been blessed with. Growing up with both of my parents alive and happily married, a wonderful man I am so grateful to be able to call my husband for over 25 years, three exceptional, healthy children, along with the very precious people God has brought into my life to feed into and guide me, are all huge blessings. To top it off, there are things like housing, cars, food, and clothing. The list goes on and on. For me to sit down and think of things I wanted felt like being on the verge of greediness.

Then, came my feelings regarding dream boards. Not because dreaming was wrong, but because I misunderstood how God fits into the process. So many people talk about how if you put your dreams on your board and paste it everywhere, so it's always in front of you, you will manifest it into reality. Wait a minute...if anything is manifesting, it's God and only God. That was another hurdle that kept me from dreaming and instead just setting my mind on what I needed to accomplish and taking the actions it took to get me there.

Have you found yourself in my shoes?

My friend, Melissa, gave me some things to try. One was making a list of 100 things I wanted. The struggle? Wrapping my head around the idea that it's not a list of 100 MATERIAL things. I remember her telling me how, at one point in her life, she just wanted a job where she could wear nice clothes. With a clearer understanding of what my list could include, how I wanted to feel, what I wanted to experience, and how I could help others, I was much more drawn to it.

Melissa also asked me about journaling. She was wondering if I had ever tried dream journaling. Maybe it was a tool God could use to help me begin again. Of course, I should invite God into the process. Just spend some time with Him and start journaling, describing how I would like things to look, feel, smell, etc. I could imagine myself in the scene and tell everything about it. He wants to give me the desires of my heart. After all, He is the One who created me and placed those desires there. I needed to recognize that the dreams I have don't always have to include me being the beneficiary.

So, when I received the perfect blue journal with a heart-shaped cover in the mail, I knew exactly who it was from and what I was meant to do with it. I sat down in my reading chair with my glass of ice water, favorite pen, and my new, blue journal. After a short prayer for guidance and to open my heart to the dreams and desires He had placed there, I began journaling with God, writing everything that came to mind. I began to describe my future, paying attention to even the smallest details.

It was right there, in my chair, where I took my first step in beginning to discover the desires of my heart—desires the One who loves me most so lovingly placed in me before I was ever born.

Somewhere along the way, many of us learned how to survive well but forgot how to imagine with God. Responsibility replaced hope. Discipline crowded out delight. And dreaming began to feel unnecessary, unrealistic, or even selfish.

But God did not place desires in your heart by accident. He is not surprised by them, threatened by them, or disappointed in them. He is the Author of them. Learning to dream again is not about wanting more for yourself; it's about trusting God enough to believe He still has more He wants to do *through* you.

I have a sticky note on my desk, reminding me that somewhere, someone is waiting for me to step into your calling so they can be blessed through you.

Learning to Dream Again

Grab a journal, a pen, and something to drink. Find a place where you feel inspired, like your favorite place in nature or a favorite room in your home. Soft worship music is something I love to add, especially when I am indoors.

1. Start with a simple prayer.

Dear Heavenly Father, I am sorry I have let the busyness of life keep me from taking time to recognize my heart's desires. One of the ways I want to honor You, Lord, is by acknowledging and even pursuing those dreams and desires, knowing it's You who carefully placed them there. Please help me be aware of even the most minor details You bring to mind as I journal with You now. Thank you for Your patience with me and for helping me to learn to dream again. In Jesus' precious name I pray. Amen.

2. Just Write.

When I first started writing this book, I remember Cathy telling me to "Just write." It's a simple phrase to remind me, especially when journaling, that one of the most essential things is to let the words flow. Don't worry about what you are writing, the words, the grammar. It's a little reminder to keep my head out of the writing and let the words flow.

3. Topics (complete these prompts)

Describe a day you are looking forward to.

Write about a day in your life three, five, ten years from now.

4. Describe the perfect job/business.

5. It's in the details.

Remember that the emotion is in the details. What is the weather like? How does it make you feel when the sun is shining on your face? As you walk through the garden, what are you smelling, hearing, and seeing? How does it make you feel?

Be specific as you begin to dream with God.

6. Release the outcome.

Remember, dreaming with God isn't about manifesting or controlling the future. It's about relationship, trust, and obedience. Some dreams may be for you. Others may be seeds meant to bless people you haven't met yet.

It takes courage, not childishness, to learn to dream again. This act may well be the first step in uncovering the desires God placed in your heart long before you developed the practicalities of adult life.

Verses

Psalm 37:4 (NASB)
"Delight yourself in the Lord; And He will give you the desires of your heart."

Hebrews 11:1 (ESV)
"Now faith is the assurance of things hoped for, the conviction of things not seen."

SIXTEEN

The Journey Continues

If you have made it this far, you know things about my life that I never would have thought I would openly mention. You've seen the parts I once shoved into the corners, hoping I could pretend they didn't exist and everything would somehow be okay.

But somewhere along the way, something began to shift.

God began opening my eyes to see how the pain I had tried to hide was still shaping my life. I started to recognize the connection between my overreactions and the broken places I had tried so hard to ignore.

For me, healing didn't happen all at once. It unfolded slowly, step by step, as God gently revealed truth and invited me to see my story through His eyes. And somewhere along the way, through the pages of this book, I believe something may have begun to shift in you too.

Maybe you're starting to recognize where God has been present in your story. Maybe you're beginning to see yourself through His eyes instead of through the labels life has placed on you. Or maybe change and hope is just beginning to appear quietly, like daffodils pushing through the early spring ground, reminding you that a new season is on the way.

Wherever God met you in these pages, I pray one truth has settled deep in your heart:

You may have been broken, but you were never meant to stay that way.

God is the God of restoration. And when He restores something, He doesn't simply return it to what it was before. He makes it stronger. I know this to be true. God can heal every broken place if we are brave enough to expose our wounds and trust Him.

Throughout these pages, you've seen pieces of my story—the fear, the doubt, and the seasons when I felt small and unqualified—the brokenness the enemy used to convince me that I wasn't enough. I lived this way for years, but God had a different plan.

What I once saw as weakness, He now uses as strength. What I once tried to hide, He now uses to help others heal. And what once felt like the end of my story turned out to be the beginning of something far greater.

This is what God does. He takes the broken pieces and builds something beautiful. And here is the part that surprised me the most:

Healing is not the destination. It's the beginning of a new journey.

We will never reach the final destination this side of heaven, but when we follow God's lead, we continue to grow in and through Him. His ways are so much better.

What we discover along the journey is that God truly does have plans for our lives—plans far greater than anything we could imagine on our own.

And you know what else I have learned along the way? The journey with God is never boring! Just when I think I understand where He is leading me, a fork appears in the tracks. Suddenly, there's a turn I never expected. I often laugh and say, "God definitely has a sense of humor."

But the best part? When I finally learned that God delights in me, I began to enjoy every curve and unexpected turn. Because now I truly believe that God's plans for my life are good. A settled confidence has replaced fear. The things I hope to accomplish, the people I want to impact, and the legacy I want to leave will be far greater with God leading the way.

Sure, there will still be bumps, and there will definitely be valleys. But I'm no longer afraid of them because God is still at the controls.

And every time He has led me through a valley, I have come out the other side stronger, braver, and more certain that the journey is worth it. That's when I recognized a shift within me. The shift? I found purpose in my pain.

A quiet strength came from realizing that God wasn't only healing me, He was also inviting me to share my story so others could see Him in theirs and find healing too. A new desire began to grow in my heart—to help women break free from the chains of their past and discover who God truly says they are. It felt like a small flame at first. But the more I shared my story, the more I saw something beautiful happen. I began to realize something powerful: healing grows stronger in a community.

Just like a trainyard where tracks from many different places come together, our lives were never meant to run on isolated rails. Community is the trainyard of our lives. Even though we may not all share the same destination, we are stronger when we walk together.

And as I watched God bring women's stories together—healing happening, courage growing, faith deepening—I began to realize something beautiful was being formed.

And from that realization, my community of women called Unshakable was born. It's a place where we rise in courage, faith, and wholeness—together. A place where we grow in our identity in Christ. Where we strengthen our faith. Where we step into our purpose. And where we learn to care for the health of the bodies God entrusted to us.

Does becoming Unshakable mean we have a perfect life? No, it's about walking so closely with God and surrounding ourselves with the right people that nothing the world throws our way can shake who we know we are. When we live from that place, we walk in confidence and boldness. Not because we have everything figured out, but because we know who we are. And more importantly, we know *whose* we are.

The Creator of all things delights in us. He delights in me, and He delights in you too. And the plans He has for your life are greater than you can imagine.

God is still writing your story. The same God who met me in my broken places is walking beside you right now. And if you allow Him, He will take every piece of your story—the pain, the healing, the unexpected turns—and weave them into something far more beautiful than you could imagine. I wonder what miracle God has waiting on the other side of your restoration?

Your brokenness may have been inevitable in this fallen world, but you were created to step into courage! I know you can go from *Broken to Brave* because Jesus paid the price for your healing. And if, somewhere along your journey, you feel God nudging you toward deeper healing, faith, and purpose, I would be honored to walk part of that journey with you in the Unshakable community. Because our journeys are meant to be shared.

And the most beautiful chapters of your story are yet to come, and I can't wait to watch them unfold.

Acknowledgements

This book exists because God met me where I was and walked with me every step of the way.

Krista, I'm thankful Cathy connected us. Thank you for bringing this book from my messy first draft to the book we have in our hands today.

Cathy, I am so grateful God gave me you to help uncover the things I had buried so deeply that I could pretend they didn't exist.

Melissa, thank you for being an example of pure joy and for showing me that radical action is no big deal—as long as I have enough deodorant.

Dad and Mom, thank you for doing your best and working so hard to provide for us.

Nathan, my amazing husband, I will never doubt that God placed you in my life at precisely the right moment. Thank you for finding me in my brokenness, for staying by my side, and for loving me despite it.

Rachael, Zachary, and Ethan, you made me a mom—one of the greatest blessings I never knew I needed. Never forget how much I love you.

And to everyone reading this book, I pray you find that place of intimacy with God, because there is no greater gift than walking through this life with Him at the controls.

Author Bio

Laura Horsch is a speaker, entrepreneur, and the founder of Laura's Legacy and the Unshakable Movement, a growing community helping women rise bold, faithful, whole, and unshakable—together. Through her message of faith, health, identity, and purpose, Laura has impacted more than 7,500 women, guiding them toward healing, freedom, and lasting change through natural solutions and faith-driven mentorship.

Laura's work is shaped by her own journey of healing, faith, and transformation. What began as a commitment to radical obedience and deeper intimacy with God grew into a calling to walk alongside women who are ready to stop striving and start living from a place of wholeness and truth.

She has spoken on a variety of stages, appeared as a guest on multiple podcasts, and was nominated for Recruiter of the Year within a global wellness company. Her leadership has earned her incentive trips to Sweden, Norway, Thailand, Bali, and Mexico. Laura is also a contributing author to The Legacy Collective, a collaborative book featuring an intimate group of top women leaders in the network marketing industry.

At the heart of her work is a passion for helping women rediscover their worth, renew their health, and create income from home aligned with their faith and family.

Laura lives in Minnesota with her husband of 25 years and is a proud mom to three young-adult children. Her mission is to remind women they were created for more—and that even in their most broken places, God is still writing a story of courage, healing, and purpose.

www.LauraHorsch.co

Need a trainer or speaker for your upcoming women's event? Looking for interesting, caring guests for your podcast?

Speaker, author, and entrepreneur Laura Horsch is available for interviews, conferences, trainings, and events!

Laura's Signature Messages/Talks:

- *Broken to Brave: Allowing God to Heal the Broken Places and Becoming Who He Created You to Be*
- *Running on Empty: Empowering Women to Take Back Their Health*

For speaking and interview inquiries, please contact Laura now at:
Laura@LauraHorsch.co

@Laurahorsch

Laura Horsch

@laurahorsch

Continue the Journey

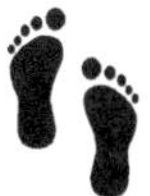

If something in these pages stirred your heart, don't stop here.
God is not finished with your story.

To help you see what it looks like to walk in confidence in who you are in Christ, I created a free guide just for you called:

Declarations for Unshakable Confidence
Speak truth. Silence doubt. Walk boldly.

Inside, you'll find simple, faith-filled declarations, Scripture, and prompts to help you step fully into who God created you to be.

👉 Download your free guide:
www.LauraHorsch.co/confidence

If you'd like to stay connected, explore more resources, or see what I'm currently working on, you can visit:
www.LauraHorsch.co

You can also connect with me on social media.
I look forward to hearing from you!

www.ingramcontent.com/pod-product-compliance
Lightning Source LLC
LaVergne TN
LVHW010839120826
845149LV00017B/3311

9798995625803